MW00881453

the MIRACLE

WORKER'S

Handbook

Affirmative Prayer and Essays

to Activate Grace, Love, Healing, Miracles and the Law of Attraction.

JACOB GLASS

DEDICATION

With Love to these Three:
Tom & Norma Belle Glass & Susie Lear

Also by Jacob Glass

Invocations: Calling Forth the Light That Heals
The Crabby Angels Chronicles
Starve a Bully, Feed a Champion
You Were Born for Greatness

Epigraph

"Prayer is the medium of miracles." – A Course in Miracles

TABLE OF CONTENTS

Acknowledgments

I want to take this opportunity to thank the Religious Science Churches/Spiritual Centers, Unity Churches and the Miracle Distribution Center for inviting and allowing me to come and do my thing with them. A huge thank you to all those who write me with encouraging words about my books and blogs – you keep me joyfully writing and I am happy to be a part of your spiritual path.

The generous tithes and donations of my readers and listeners have helped to establish this wonderful Joy Academy which has grown and grown for over 25 years now. The best is yet to come and I am so grateful and humbled by your wonderful generosity and kindness.

<u>INTRODUCTION</u>

"You're the reason he'll never amount to anything! Of course the other kids don't want him around. He doesn't even dress like the other boys. You'll be taking care of him the rest of his life."

The words stung me as they filtered through the wall between my parents bedroom and my own. I wasn't supposed to be able to hear the accusations my mother hurled at my father, but angry words often carry over a greater distance than we realize.

I pushed the pillows over my head and scrunched down under the cover, deeper and deeper into darkness where it was safe and quiet. Well, not exactly quiet. The words rang out in my ears over and over again, louder and louder. Words that roared through my stomach like a runaway train. My whole body vibrating before going into shutdown.

I thought, *"Why can't everyone leave me alone? I hate this town. I hate feeling this way. What's wrong with me? Why can't anyone love me? Why can't I do anything right? I have to get away from here and find someplace where I won't be hurt anymore. Someplace where I'll fit in and people will accept me."*

Yet long after I had left that house and the greenery of rural Pennsylvania, I would still hear those words and so many others haunting me as I went from town to town, person to person. It seemed that I couldn't outrun them no matter how hard I tried.

My mother was right, I didn't fit in anywhere. What I hadn't anticipated when I left, was that twenty years later I would still be hearing those agonizing words, *"Never amount to anything. Different. Failure. Quitter."* As a teenager the voice brought pain, but as an adult, the voice took on a particularly ugly and viscous tone that was often unbearable. It had become unbearable because now the voice was my own.

I'd spent most of my youth escaping into fantasy. My Catholic school upbringing equated suffering with sainthood and so it was easy for me to slip into a dream-world where my persecution was merely proof of my holiness. I foolishly told myself that if I didn't fit in it was because I was different in the way that all truly special people are different. I was too skinny and afraid to participate in sports and too cripplingly shy to do much else. I was certain that I was the only person who felt so alone. Often I imagined myself standing in front of a huge picture window, on the outside looking in at the rest of the world.

I became an expert at hiding in plain sight. Being noticed was painful. Being noticed often meant not only verbal abuse, but many times physical violence. Expressing any emotion, particularly anger, brought almost immediate pain. School was a place where I would be hit, spat on, humiliated and beaten up. Even teachers were not beyond ridiculing me and once a shop teacher even yanked on my hair until my scalp bled and my glasses flew off my face and across the room. Yet in spite of it all I desperately wanted someone to notice what was good in me.

I learned to keep secrets from my family. It was too humiliating to let them know how horrible things were. How could I tell them that I was tormented daily, called names and ridiculed. I didn't want them to be disappointed or more worried than they already were. The truth is I was afraid that maybe I *never would amount to anything*. Maybe everyone was right about me. Maybe I was nothing. Besides, I knew there was nothing they could do to change things. I saw first hand the way this world responds to anyone who is different in any way. If I didn't even feel safe to tell my mother that I was angry, how in the world could I tell her that I was gay?

By the time I reached the age of 23 I had moved to San Diego, California and began to come to terms with my sexuality. Yet something told me that this was only part of the turmoil that I was experiencing. There was more going on than the issue of who I loved or even the prejudices of society against being gay. I was having problems in all of my relationships and in every area of my life. As I looked around I noticed that most of my straight friends were as messed up as I was. It wasn't a matter of sexuality. That was just a smokescreen. I began to notice that a lot of people had the same critical voice in their heads that I had in mine. It told them that they were worthless or that other people were worthless. It held them back in crucial areas of creativity and expression. It victimized them as it victimized me. We all had different ways of keeping the voice down, drinking, drugs, food, sex, overworking, anything but face those horrible words.

I wanted so much out of life, yet I felt helpless to change myself or my situation. I had a deep faith in God, but no faith in myself. It wasn't enough anymore just to pray that things would get better. There had to be a better way. I had begun to beg God for help.

After a miserable summer of desperation and unanswered prayers, in 1983 I sat in a deep depression watching TV on a Sunday morning. I flipped through the channels searching for some inspiration for the coming week. What I found changed my life forever. A beautiful, tan, blonde woman, named Terry Cole-Whittaker was giving a sermon based on a book called "A Course In Miracles". She hadn't written the book, but she was using it in her teaching and in her own life. She also quoted from the Bible but, in a down to earth and very psychologically hip manner. She was funny and fun. She scared me. I figured she was some trippy California cult leader. And what was she so happy about? Still, for the next few months I found myself tuning in each week to watch her. She challenged me. She challenged my belief systems and said that I was not a victim but that I could actively seek to change my life by first changing the nature of my thinking. When she talked about God, it was the God I'd believed in and known as a child. This God loved me unconditionally and wasn't angry at me. This was the God I remembered and knew in my heart. I began to feel different. I began to experience my feelings more. Something was happening inside of me at last.

A few months later I began attending Terry's church services and took a class she was teaching that used this "miracles" book and based on the teachings of Ernest Holmes who'd written a book on "The Science of Mind." I remember sitting down to read these rather large books and having a sense of peace wash over me. As I read I felt the familiarity of the words, not like something new, but like something I had always known but had forgotten. This is not to say that the information in the books did not completely disrupt my old thought system. I was being asked to question every belief I had about myself, God and the entire world. Obviously this was not a quick fix. No easy answers or shortcuts; but I knew it was my way out of the torment that went on inside me. I knew that there was a place inside of me where I would find the peace and love I'd been searching for so desperately, the place A Course In Miracles calls, A Place of Refuge.

Well, it's many years later now and though I can't say that I am never afraid or upset, I can say that I am happy in a way that is deeper than the external kind of happiness I dreamed of as a young boy. It hasn't been easy, but it's been worth every minute. I now lecture to large and small groups of people throughout Southern California. I've lectured to and counseled everyone from major Hollywood celebrities to secretaries and ex-convicts. My own interpretation of spiritual principles is not for everyone. There are those who find me too offensive or controversial because of my street language or the topics I choose. Some cannot get beyond my sexuality or even the way that I look. Ultimately, none of these things matter to me. My goal is to make available the same message that others have so generously passed on to me. Every time I have been down on my knees asking God to guide me I have always been sent the messenger whom I could most easily understand. Dear Reader, if you understand what I am writing, then I am writing this for you.

Jacob Glass
1999

<u>WHAT IS PRAYER TREATMENT?</u>

My earliest memory of praying is in the bedroom I shared with my parents in the attic of my childhood home in rural Pennsylvania. From my parents bed, which was across the room from mine, my mother would listen to make sure I got it right as I said, *"Now I lay me down to sleep, I pray the Lord my soul to keep, if I should die before I wake, I pray the Lord my soul to take."* It scared me a bit to think that it was possible that I might die in my sleep.

Back then I thought God was someone "up there" looking down on me, watching and deciding who lived and who died. I suppose my prayers were more like bargaining than communing with the Divine. My motivation had more to do with guilt and fear than a deep love for God. I definitely believed in an Old Testament kind of God; angry and judgmental. In retrospect, it's easy to recognize that feelings of fear and guilt do not lead to closeness nor open honest communication.

Until my mid-twenties my prayers consisted mostly of either begging God to get me out of trouble I'd gotten myself into or asking to be saved from some anxiety-provoking future event. Having more to do with superstition than spirituality, I was treating God like a lucky penny.

As my own understanding of the spiritual principles of life has changed, so has the nature of my prayers. The most important aspect of my prayers now is the request that God's will be done. I think of it as the safety clause of all prayers. It keeps me from putting my self-initiated plans before the plans of God. It guarantees my ultimate happiness even if the outcome of circumstances does not fit my particular pictures.

But, for me personally, just the phrase *"God's will be done"* is not enough to bring me peace all the time. I have to ask myself, do I believe that God's will is that I be happy? Do I trust that God is a loving God? Do I have faith in that love even when circumstances do not reflect it in this moment? This is why the form of prayers you'll be reading are called "affirmative prayers". Affirmative prayer assumes and declares the innate goodness of God and the Universe. It claims that God is right here and right now. They are often also called "Prayer Treatment" – as a medical practitioner would treat an illness with medication, etc., a spiritual practitioner treats the mind with prayer treatment.

Like the Psalms of David, which were often songs of praise, these prayers are meant to open our hearts to God's love and blessings. *"The Lord is my shepherd; I shall not want. He maketh me to lie down in green pastures: He leadeth me beside the still waters. He restoreth my soul: he leadeth me on the paths of righteousness for his name's sake."* This is the kind of prayer we are learning to master. We trust in God's will and we are not afraid to say specifically how good that will is; for us and for all the world.

Prayer can be like the warm overstuffed comforter we wrap ourselves in on a rainy day or it can be the scrap of wood we cling to adrift in a vast cold ocean as we watch the Titanic sink from view.

Real prayer is a relationship, it is not static. True prayer is an ever-evolving, living, breathing relationship between our deepest self and the universal forces. In it's most profound form it is the relationship with the Divine. At other times it is the relationship with the worldly forces of fear and sacrifice. Nearly every thought we have is some kind of prayer. Like any relationship, it grows from careful attention and cultivation or it withers & dies from lack of care.

There is no communication like the communication that we call prayer. It transcends and uplifts when we open ourselves to it's mystical powers. It is as equally accessible to the king as it is to the slave. God is no respecter of persons and divine love is equally poured out to all who care to make contact with high intention. Yet, we waste the power if we think that prayer is simply a way of getting something. Prayer is most certainly a means to an end, but the end is so much more significant than tangible things. Too many of us go to the Master of all Creation, the limitless Maker of All Things and we settle for crumbs.

To settle for crumbs is to cherish the package instead of the gift that is carefully laid inside. While it may be true that cars, mates, money and "things" can come from prayer, they never really satisfy for long. There is always the need for the next thing. Our thirst is never quenched because we ask for shabby substitutes of the real living waters.

The simple truth is that we live in an abundant universe that was set up to support us all. There are more than enough resources for everyone on the earth to live like millionaires for their entire lives. Yet, we don't all live truly abundant lives because of our obsession with having more. There are those who "have" who do not understand that the greatest abundance comes from sharing what you have. There are those who "have not" who simply resent those who have and continue to think they are victimized by their situation. Both are living under a worldly delusion.

If we could only understand that our desire for things, or for endless acknowledgment and for our desires to be met is simply a yearning for God. What we really desire is God . . . but, God is not some far off stranger. God resides in everyone we meet and we miss the Divine as we pass people by every day. We walk right past the hidden Christ while looking for a new pair of shoes that might be a temporary mood-elevator. We ignore the suffering while we pray for a nicer apartment.

Now, there is nothing wrong with having a nicer apartment. Certainly every one of us has the right to have our basic needs of food, shelter and medical care met. And not just to scrape by either but to really flourish in this life. And of course if a man is hungry and jobless then we should most certainly tell him to pray that his physical needs be met by divine action . . . and we should join with him in prayer . . . and then after we pray, we should allow God to use us personally to take whatever action we can or seems most right and helpful to that man at that moment. For this much is certain; prayer works, but it works most often through people. It is a divine and mystical action but it comes quite beautifully through the human vessel. Therefore, the prayer *"God use me"* is one of the most effective requests we can make.

Still, I do not wish to encourage anyone to be a "spiritual nitwit" either. There are those who walk the earth thinking they are unattached servants of the Lord who really have just not taken responsibility for their own lives and so other people end up becoming responsible for them. This is not God's will. That is why I say if you need rent money then don't hesitate to pray for rent money. Even Jesus taught us to pray for our daily bread. Mother Theresa was a woman of prayer but, also a woman of action. I encourage people to do their prayer work being specific about their needs if in a very needful state of mind, but, do it with an eye toward the day when these temporary situations will be healed and know that the real prayer then is *"Lord, I am yours. Lead me in Your gentle ways and make my life a living testament to the goodness and grace of God. Take my hands and feet and voice and let them serve You."*

We should approach prayer as naturally as an intimate conversation with a dear friend; with love, respect and honesty. As with any relationship, it grows and changes over time and blossoms with careful attention. In loving relationships there is honest sharing followed by quiet listening. We must not pray "at God". At the end of each prayer, spend time opening up to feel the gentle response which comes.

My purpose in writing this little volume is to give you a spiritual companion on your journey through the rigors and challenges of daily life. Each prayer has been carefully crafted to gently lift you up in consciousness to the place of Divine Aid. I hope you will keep it nearby; in your car, purse, backpack, briefcase or by the bed. My prayer is that you will develop a relationship with these prayers that will expand and enliven your own prayers. The more that you use it the more deeply the words will sink into your memory and your subconscious mind. Eventually it will become a habit to think the highest most holy thoughts all day long.

WHERE IS YOUR FAITH?

I could feel that beginning tickle of a scratchy throat. I had a lecture to give in two hours and I wasn't looking forward to speaking for an hour when I was already starting to feel myself falter. My friend Diane sat across from me at the kitchen table and I told her that I hoped I was not catching my god-son's cold. Without even taking a beat she looked up and said, *"Where is your faith?"*

It was very simply said with no judgment and I knew she wasn't expecting an answer. It wasn't really a question so much as a reminder. Where was my faith? Did I have faith in the existence and danger of germs that I needed to defend myself against? At that moment, yes, that is where my faith was placed. But, her simple words put things back in proper order. I had the choice of where to place my faith; faith in the Divine Presence within me, or faith in the physical world of appearances. My return to faith in God was not that I would not get sick, but rather the realization that what I needed to be saved from was the thought that that would be a bad thing.

People will sometimes tell you in times of trouble, *"You're never given more than you can handle."* This is not my experience nor is it the experience of millions of other people who suffer and die every day. It seems to me that the deeper truth is that I am never given more than *God-within-me* can handle.

So this *"where is your faith"* is a good question. In fact, it is one of the best questions you can ask yourself. I have asked it of myself thousands of times since that day and always it returns me to awareness of the divine.

The question is good because it implies a truth which is this; your faith is always somewhere. You are never bereft of faith. It is sometimes simply misplaced though - yes that is it, "mis-placed" - placed where it does not belong.

Faith itself is a constant attribute of consciousness. However, where faith resides is what changes and fluctuates. Sometimes our faith is in God, the divine, the goodness of life, and sometimes it is in our money, our intelligence, our physical strength or our talents. Perhaps we put our faith in the government or in the law to protect and care for us. Generally speaking even the most religious among us are unaware of our tendency to have faith in our own strength. Usually we are running the show - and often with little real success.

The world we see all around us encourages us to put our faith in fear although it names this fear "knowledge". Every day the newspapers and television keep us acutely aware of the danger that lurks everywhere, even in our own homes. In many ways we bow down to and worship the gods of fear and defense. Over and over we are taught by the voices of fear how to defend ourselves against whatever enemy confronts us. Our lives have become warzones.

In these days of constant change and uncertainty there are those who are forever claiming we are in the last days or the end-times. The mind is fascinated and yet often paralyzed by the idea of enemies "out there" who are out to get us. What we haven't realized is that we created these enemies through our own fearful thoughts and just as that realm gave birth to the enemy it can just as surely give rise to thoughts of a savior.

What does this savior save us from? In many ways we are saved from our own cleverness, which has too often been used against us. Experience is teaching us that our fighting gets us nowhere. It's obvious that the war on drugs, the war on poverty, the war on germs and crime have all made the opponents stronger and more clever. Even some germs and diseases are getting stronger because of antibiotics.

What we fight against becomes stronger because it feeds on our attention. That is why we are told in scripture to *"resist not evil"* - our very resistance gives evil strength. Whatever is the object of our attention receives energy. Therefore, the answer has to be a way of starving the enemy of attention and turning instead toward the light. The answer is a new way of thinking which then gives rise to another way of being and doing - it dawns first in the mind and then radiates outward.

This doesn't mean we pretend that there are no problems or that we ignore the suffering of others. Not at all. In fact, the more time we spend in relationship with divine thinking the more we grow in compassion and understanding. Ultimately our faith in divine love increases each time we offer ourselves as servants of that love here on earth. Our own faith, our own convictions are strengthened by giving away what has been given to us. Therefore, we are not just turning away from darkness, we are actually turning to the Light and actively using our hands, our feet and our voices to increase the forces of goodness and beneficence and when enough of us join the ranks of the Light-bearers, the world is literally overtaken by that Light and the darkness is cast out.

What this means is that there is less time fighting the war against poverty and more time spent creating a society of abundance for everyone; there is less time spent fighting new germs and illnesses and more time spent awakening the body's own healing immune system, there is more time spent increasing human dignity and self-worth and less time fighting drugs. This is what the life of prayer and faith will and does bring.

Now it is our task to awaken to how much of our time is spent in a constant prayer of fear and dread and how much time is spent in a prayer to a Higher Power which can deliver us from all fear and pain through the transforming of our minds. There have been times when I have written *"where is your faith?"* on post-its and put them up on my door to see as I leave the house, in my car to remember as I am driving in Los Angeles traffic, and on my computer screen to keep as my mantra all through the day.

Ultimately our faith is always justified one way or another. It's important that we recognize that Jesus often told those he healed that it was their faith that made them whole. Jesus healed the willing. People came to him for this reason and believed with all their hearts that he could perform a miracle. Jesus never tried to convince anyone who did not want the gift. He merely made it available to those who had the faith to receive it. We have free will as to what we will place our faith and belief in, although many voices in the world are constantly trying to sway our faith their way.

Where is your faith right now? Where have you placed it? Is that the world you want to live in today? Choose you this day what faith you will serve today for it will most surely come back to serve you.

The
Prayers

DAILY AFFIRMATIVE PRAYER

God is with me now. He has a plan for my life.
I believe in the power of God. I believe in miracles.
I believe in the radical action of God's love here on earth.
There is no opposite to this power –
it flows from God through me now.
God uses my hands, my feet,
and my voice this day to do His Will.
All good is effortlessly drawn to me today.
I cannot fail to be at the right place at the right time.
There is limitless good – more than enough for everyone.
All fear and negativity are washed clean from me now.
There is no need to worry or rush –
the Universe has perfect timing.
I embrace this new day and the miracles it brings.
I am a radiant beam of Light which attracts friends,
love, success, good health, and joy.
I am not afraid to be happy today. I am not afraid of love.
Love and acknowledgment shine on me
from all directions today.
People are drawn to me and love to
assist me in truly helpful ways.
My business and all my affairs are run by Divine Intelligence.
I always have more than enough money to
ay all my bills and live an abundant lifestyle.
This is a rich season of Divine Harvest.
My body radiates good health and energy
as this is the pure reflection of God's love.
I am never alone nor lonely for my
brother Jesus is here beside me.
I breathe life in deeply and I am relaxed and at peace.
My mind is clear and my heart is full of love for all of life.
Nothing wavers me from my truth today.
All that I need is given me.
I have no lack of any good thing.
There is a power in me.

I have my Father's power to heal and reveal.
My relationships are loving and intimate.
My appetites are made right by the
principle of perfect assimilation.
Every organ and cell of my body is
alive with Divine Intelligence.
This intelligence keeps the flow of
energy and health at an optimum.
I maintain my perfect weight and
desire the best foods and exercise.
All mental, physical and emotional habits which are not of a
sweet and loving nature now drop from my atmosphere.
I deserve love and companionship and I am open
to receive that love now in whatever forms are best.
The Universe has chosen the right people and
they are welcomed by me now.
I have loving intimate relationships and I am happy.
My family and loved ones are surrounded by
the white light of Divine Protection.
I am thankful to the Father for all this good and for my life.
I step back now and allow the Universe to do the work.
I do not interfere nor doubt.
I trust that it is done and so it is. Amen

A Prayer for The Children Of The World

The Divine Father Mother Presence is
now blessing all the children of the world.
Each one is now held safely in the arms of
an angel of God who guides and protects
them all through the day and night.
All parents everywhere are now being filled
with loving-kindness, patience and wisdom.
All the resources necessary to raise
a healthy, happy and successful child

are now being drawn into their lives.
There are more than enough resources in the
Universe to care for all the children of the world
and even now the leaders and citizens of
every country and nation are being Divinely
guided and supported to care for the health,
educational, spiritual, financial
and emotional needs of the world's youth.
Every school, park, playground and home
is protected and held perfectly
in the hands of God.
Here and now I give God my hands, my feet and
my voice to be used to make the world a safer
and more wonderful place for all
children to grow and thrive in.
I allow myself to be used in the service of
helping to raise up a society of healthy and happy adults.
I send out my loving thoughts now as a
beacon of light which shines outward
into every street of the world, blanketing the
globe with God's love and safety.
We are all healed together.
The family, whatever form it takes,
is restored by Divine Love this very day.
I thank You Lord for hearing my prayer
and for the manifestations of good which now
follow - I release this prayer to You now in
full faith knowing that it is done by Your
Holy Spirit for the highest good of all concerned.
And so it is. Amen

PRAYER FOR MY DAUGHTER

Great Divine Spirit, bless this child of mine.
I know that this precious girl was sent
from the Light and is lovingly held by the Angels.
I am merely a vessel through which God's love flows.
I release my own goals and agendas for this child
that she might find her own great destiny.
Even now everything that is good, beautiful and holy
is being irresistibly drawn to her.
May she have everything needed to live a life of
joy, success and great happiness.
Love is her natural state of being and I know that God is the
Source of all her needs. I release her to You now.
May I be here when she needs me but not
squelch her expression by following too closely.
Help me to balance freedom and responsibility.
May she grow into the fullness of her femininity.
May she cultivate the friendships of other women.
May she find her own center of power within and
not seek in the world for her approval.
Let her never shrink from her own intelligence.
May she find her place in the world.
May she love greatly and be loved in return.
May she love and accept her body as it is and as it is not.
May she grow in physical strength and health.
May her mind and eyes be open that she may
grow in wisdom and compassion.
May the world be blessed for her having been here.
Thank You for this precious precious gift.
Amen

PRAYER FOR MY SON

Father Mother God, embrace my Son in Your Love.
I place him in Your hands now that he may walk in Light.
Strengthen his heart and mind and keep him safe from harm.
May he grow into the man You would have him be.
May he be a man of honor, compassion and truth.
Keep him strong in faith that he may be guided
only by Your Voice within him.
Strengthen his body but, may his strength
never be used in anger.
May compassion temper his judgment.
Open his mind that he may have empathy and patience
with those whose views are different from his own.
Let him never carry his burdens alone nor
think it weak to ask for help.
Source him and be his supply that he may prosper & succeed.
Help him to keep the adventurous heart of a boy
but with the maturity of a man.
May he have a tender heart and a keen mind.
May his work be a joy to him.
May he laugh every day but never at the expense of another.
May he understand the importance of family.
May he honor women and his fellow man.
Help me Lord, to hold the light for him
without my shadow interfering with his path.
I entrust him into Your care.
Thank You for this gift.
May he bless the world.
Amen

AFFIRMATIVE PRAYER FOR CHILDREN TO SAY

God placed in me a beautiful light,
That guides and protects me all day and all night.
I am His child and am filled
with His love,
And angels surround me
below and above.
I know I'm exactly who
I'm supposed to be,
Everyone loves me for
just being me.
Thank You God for
watching over our family.
Amen

AFFIRMATIVE PRAYER FOR YOUNG PEOPLE & TEENAGERS

I am as God created me and I am exactly
who and what I was meant to be.
There is a beautiful spirit within me that holds
and protects me all through the day and night.
Nothing and no one can diminish this perfect Spirit inside me.
There are no words nor actions from outside of me that can
change this beautiful beam of light which I am.
I came to Earth to be just who and what I am and
I have a wonderful job to do.
All that I need in order to do what I came here to do is
provided for me by Divine Substance and Supply.
I am surrounded by unseen angels who
love me and watch over me.
I am a unique person in the Universe and no one can
take my place or fill the role I came here to play.
My heart is filled with love overflowing
for myself and for those closest to me.

I am a special person and I recognize my brilliance.
I came to love the world and I have my own
unique way of making that love manifest.
I am willing to rise above all circumstances in order to accept
my part in healing the world by living with integrity, love,
honor, compassion and goodness.
Today I will not judge myself nor anyone I meet.
Today I will treat myself as a precious human treasure.
Today I will know that I matter.
Today I will tell someone else that they matter too.
Oh Lord, thank You for making me just the way I am.
I will not criticize Your work today by judging myself.
Instead, I humbly ask that You make any changes
in me that You see fit to make and I will love, honor
and adore whatever remains.
From this day on I will not harm myself in any way.
I will treat myself as a vessel of the living spirit of Love.
I will not be tempted by anyone or anything
to abuse or dishonor myself.
I surrender my relationship with
my parents and my family to You.
May we grow in love, communication and understanding.
May all our needs be provided for this very day.
Lord, help me to live in love today.
Protect me and those I love along with all the world.
Please bless my family and all families everywhere.
Shine Your light on us now.
Pour Your blessings on us.
I give my life to You.
Thank You God that this is so. Amen

PRAYER FOR OUR PARENTS

The Christ in me calls forth the Christ in my parents.
We are One in God.
I honor them now for giving birth to me.
I am grateful to God for whatever good they have given me.
I claim that I am heir to what they did right and I let go of
their mistakes.
My heart is filled with compassion.
I release my father and mother into God's care.
They are blessed and embraced by Divine Love.
All their needs are taken care of this very day.
Their bodies and health are sustained by God.
They are filled with vital energy.
Their finances come from Divine Supply.
There are limitless resources for their
abundant life, prosperity and happiness.
Joy fills their hearts and their minds are clear and calm.
They are safe from harm and free from fear.
Their good cannot be denied for it comes from God Himself.
I forgive and release my parents from the past.
I release myself from the past.
We are encircled by the light of deep forgiveness and
acceptance.
We are set free from the bondage of our past roles and are free
to be who we truly are at depth.
I let go of trying to make sense of the past.
We now step into a dynamic present.
I let go of the form and accept Divine Content.
I am grateful to God for the freedom of this healing.
And so it is.
And so I let it be.
Amen

BEDTIME PRAYER

The Divine Father Mother Presence of God
now enters my consciousness as I let go of the day.
I let go of all that went wrong and all that went right.
I now recognize my mistakes and release them into
His forgiveness. I accept with grace the lessons learned.
I let go of those who may have hurt or offended me.
I will not take my anger to bed and so I forgive as best I can.
As I sleep, all my worries dissolve and I rest in God.
I give thanks for this day.
While I sleep, my family and loved ones are
all held safely in the arms of God.
My sleep is restful and healing.
My body and mind relax and let go.
My dreams are peaceful and teach me
what God would have me know.
I invite the Angels to now enter my mind that they may
guide me to the Higher Realms of Consciousness.
My home and all who abide here are filled with
Divine love which protects us from all harm.
All are safe in His care this night.
As I turn my eyes from the outer world I am
filled with the assurance that God is in control.
May my sleep give me the rest I need that
tomorrow I may do better.
May I be made into the person that
God would have me be.
For this I am so grateful
So it is.
Amen

PREPARATION PRAYER

I relinquish all fear and control to Father Mother God.
My Holy Guide has brought me this far
and will not abandon me now.
I am not alone. I have Divine Assistance.
There is no need for fear or worry for God is here beside me.
I let go of trying to control circumstances
and surrender into His will.
All the brightest and the best within me
is brought forward this day.
The Light of God shines brightly in me
and radiates out into all I do and say.
My thoughts are high, my spirit soars
and my heart is open wide.
I breathe deeply and release all nervousness and fear.
All anxiety dissolves into Divine Confidence.
I give this situation to the Source of all good to control.
All outcomes are placed in the hands of perfect love of God.
All people, places and situations are now brought in line
with Spiritual truth. There are no obstructions to God's plan.
Nothing can delay or impede the will of God.
My body and mind are peaceful, calm and relaxed.
There is nothing to fear.
There is nothing to get - no need to make anything happen.
I let go of all resistance. I let go of all pain.
Thank You God for walking with me now.
Thank You for caring.
Thank You for the Divine Solution to all problems.
Thank You for Divine Strength to accept all things.
I release this to You now knowing that all unfolds
perfectly according to Your will for the
highest good of all concerned.
So it is.
Amen

COMPLETION PRAYER

God can heal all things.
I now surrender this experience to God.
I acknowledge myself for showing up and doing my best.
Whatever mistakes I may have made are
healed by Divine Restoration.
I forgive myself now so that God may enter my mind.
My heart is filled with forgiveness for
any mistakes that were made by another.
Christ-in-me is more powerful than any particular situation.
I am at the effect of God alone.
There is nothing to control, obsess or worry about.
God is in charge and all is well.
Divine process is at work here and
there is a plan for the greater good.
My good is never withheld from me.
I am always at choice in my perceptions and thoughts.
I choose to see things with miraculous perception.
The peace of God washes away all fear and anxiety.
I call on and claim Divine Right Action
for all aspects of this situation.
God's plan is one in which everyone wins.
I accept His plan now.
I let go of this experience now and
surrender every aspect of it to God.
If there is something still to be done
I will be told by Divine Wisdom.
All is well in the hands of God.
I slow down my thoughts.
I breathe deeply.
I relax.
I let go.
Thank You God.
Amen

PRAYER FOR THE WORLD

God is with me now. He has a plan for the world.
I believe that God is all good and everywhere present.
I believe in the power of His love here on Earth.
I believe that He wills that the planet be healed.
I now begin to see the world as God would have it be.
All life is now cradled in His loving arms.
There is no place on Earth that His light does not touch.
I now call upon His holy name to heal this world.
Divine Love is now flowing through every country and nation.
Every man, woman and child is embraced in perfect love.
There is no poverty, pain, sickness nor lack in God.
This is an abundant universe and there are more than
enough resources for everyone to have all that they need.
Every person and nation now draws to them all that they need
in order to be happy, healthy, safe and loved.
Under God's plan everyone wins and no one loses.
Greed, addictions, anger, prejudice and sickness
all dissolve in the miracle of Divine Restoration.
The need to be right is released and dissolves.
All of nature is being brought into harmony as
the plants, animals and all living things
are restored to their natural state of being.
The citizens and leaders of every nation are now
being awakened to the truth of our Oneness.
All beings everywhere are being lifted up
to their highest and best.
We recognize the sacredness of all life.
We are all healed together.
Here and now I give my life to God that I may be used as
an instrument of healing and change.
I recognize my importance in this
plan for salvation of the world.
May I do no harm. May I help wherever I can.
Use me, Lord. I am Yours.

CENTERING PRAYER

I now turn inward to the Center of
my Being where God abides.
I go the well of Infinite Goodness and Wisdom.
There is a perfect Presence within me that now radiates love
throughout my entire being - I am at home here.
I invoke and awaken the Christ Consciousness within me.
I dip into the Divine Center of Infinite Supply.
Calmness, peace and tranquility are mine.
The Father and I are One.
Nothing can pull or distract me from
the truth of the Spirit within me.
I come inside where I am sheltered
by God's love and warmth.
The Divine Presence within me now
speaks to me of who and what I am.
All through the day and night I am
reminded of the power that
is in all beings everywhere.
I choose from this moment on to see God in all things.
I now remember who I am and where I came from.
Nothing and no one can separate me from the love of God.
I am not alone for He is here beside me.
Every breath that I take heals my worried mind.
There is nothing to control. Nothing to change.
I accept the perfection of this moment just as it is.
I know that I am one with God and His voice
within me speaks to me clearly now.
I thank You Divine Father for hearing me and for the
manifestations of good which now follow.
I now release everything to the all-loving inner presence.
I surrender myself and all that I am to the Mother-Father God.
All is well. I am loved.
Thank You God.
And so it is.
Amen

<u>REMEMBER TO:</u>

Slow Down

Breathe

Relax

Let Go

RELATIONSHIP PRAYER TREATMENT FOR SINGLES

There is a bright beam of light shining
from the heart of God directly into mine.
Divine Love opens my heart like a flower in the sunlight.
I am filled with love overflowing and
I allow myself to love all people.
I am not afraid of intimate love.
My consciousness now expands to
make room for my right mate to enter.
I include this person in my world and
I deeply surrender all fears and barriers.
God now creates a relationship that is healthy, fun, loving,
supportive and based on deep abiding friendship.
I know that I deserve love and that
with God all things are possible.
There is no lack in God and none in me.
There is more than enough love for everyone.
I am not held back by any circumstances
for God is all powerful.
My age, my past, my mistakes, my frailties, my quirks and
character defects are nothing to the power of the Holy Spirit.
I am whole and complete just as I am.
Nothing can keep my good away.
I no longer attract shadow figures
from my past for I am healed and forgiven.
I release with love all my past relationships and accept their
important part in my learning and growth.
And now I am reborn. All is made right in this holy instant.
There is no need to seek for a relationship nor for a person.
My right relationship already exists in the mind of God.
My awareness now expands so that I may
recognize the answer to my prayer.
The Holy Spirit has chosen the right person and
I accept that person into my life now.
We are being drawn together by Divine Right Action.

I do not strain nor worry for I know that our relationship,
it's timing and all it's circumstances rest in God's hands.
I give thanks now as I release this to Him in full-faith knowing
that all will happen according to His will
for the highest good of all concerned.
And so it is.
Amen

RELATIONSHIP PRAYER TREATMENT FOR COUPLES

God has brought us together and
this relationship has been touched by Him.
I place it in His care. I believe that love is the greatest truth.
This relationship is a source of joy and
inspiration to us both and gratitude fills our hearts.
All that we need comes to us.
Divine Supply sustains us.
Angels surround us and support our lives.
We are safe to love and be loved.
We are free to play and laugh together.
It is safe for us to relax into this happiness.
I commit myself this day to the
highest love of which I am capable.
We are safe to share the truth without attack.
We truly know and see each other.
We are a safe space for one another.
Our love blesses and supports us.
We have been drawn together
by God's power for His purposes.
God sustains and sources every aspect of our love.
Words of praise and acknowledgment
flow freely and abundantly between us.
Intimacy, tenderness and good humor fill our conversations.
All past guilt and negative patterns
are released and we are set free.

Jealousy, envy and mistrust are washed away
and find no home in us.
All power struggles dissolve and we relax into the Divine Flow.
Trust and honesty grow daily in our hearts and minds.
We choose to focus on love and to let go of the rest.
God chooses the form which
is perfect for our ultimate happiness.
Judgments and criticism cease as we
acknowledge the best in one another.
Our physical relationship is loving, stimulating and fulfilling.
All communications are filtered through the
Divine Veil and only what is loving and true is heard.
God Himself corrects every mistake.
Patience and compassion rule our hearts.
We receive all that we give.
Thank You Lord for this precious gift.
Thank You for the blessing of this magnificent person.
Thank You for our love.
Thank You for our lives.
We are healed.
So it is.
Amen

Prayer Treatment for Career/Work

God has called me by my name and I am His.
He has a place for me in this world and
it is the place I want to be.
There is no place nor position in which
I cannot work for Him.
I now allow myself to be lifted to what He would have me do.
In all things I seek and find the glory of serving God
by serving the people who are sent to me.
This day, right now I am in my right place
for this particular day.

I am happy and humbled that I may be of use for
however long this work serves His purposes.
I recognize that God's will is that I be happy, loved and
successful. I surrender into His will now.
That which I love to do brings me great joy, prosperity,
satisfaction and a sense of accomplishment.
Spirit brings to me all that is mine.
I deserve a work environment in which there is mutual support
in calling forth our best talents, creativity and inner-resources.
I know that this is God's will.
All the assistance and resources to do this job with excellence
now come to me quickly and easily.
There is no strain and my atmosphere supports me in
bringing forth my highest and best.
God is the source of my supply and so I
am always well compensated for my work.
My right work thrives and flourishes.
My work is unaffected by current
economic changes and trends.
My stability rests on Divine Economics.
There is an ever-expanding and limitless inflow of good.
Love permeates my thoughts, words and actions and
this is an attractive energy.
My work is appreciated and acknowledged.
I let go of all past work experiences
and beliefs about my career.
I let go of what other people think
for I care only what God thinks.
I know that I have Divine Approval.
I allow myself to receive my good.
I am so happy to be given this opportunity to serve in joy.
Thank You God. Thank You God. Thank You God.
Amen

Physical Healing Prayer Treatment

There is a Divine Physician within me.
Eternal wisdom and healing abide in me.
I place my body in the care of the Supreme Intelligence.
This Intelligence is in every living thing that exists and
It exists in me now.
It perfectly runs my body to it's fullest potential.
This Intelligence is the same power that
Jesus used to heal the sick and the dead.
I call on that Power now to make Itself known in me.
Right now Divine Love is coursing through my veins into my
organs and into every cell of my body.
Every breath I take relaxes my muscles, eases
all tensions and makes my mind peaceful and still.
There is nothing to strive for nor against -
no illness to resist nor condition to battle.
Whatever is happening in my body is loved
and accepted, for anything that is
not a reflection of perfect love is temporary.
Divine Intelligence knows exactly
how to run my body perfectly.
My body is healthy and fit and it feels good.
I love and bless my body just as it is and just as it is not.
It is a temporary vehicle and I appreciate
every detail the Creator made.
I allow myself to enjoy healthy foods and exercise.
All that I do contributes to my health and vitality.
I allow myself to be fully alive.
I do not use my body for safety nor to hide.
My body is free of my past emotions and thoughts.
I release any addictions or disorders for they have
no power in the presence of the Holy Spirit.
Only the laws of God apply to my health.
I forgive myself for any harm I may have done to my body
in the past - it is over now and can have no effect.
I identify myself with Spirit and not with the flesh.

I give thanks to my body for all that it has done for me.
I give thanks to God for healing it now.
And so it is.
Amen

FORGIVENESS PRAYER TREATMENT

G od is healing me now.
I can no longer weary myself with my judgments.
I call to mind those whom I feel have harmed me
or withheld from me what is mine.
Together we are released from the prison I have made for us.
I let go of who is right and who is wrong.
There is no resentment in God and none in me.
I am free in this holy moment of release as I allow God to heal
my broken heart, my frightened, angry mind and my tired soul.
I call upon His Holy Spirit to
come into me and make me whole.
I know that the Spirit within me is safe from all harm and
that everything that is mine comes to me now.
Divine Action is compelling all people, places and
circumstances to come to a happy
conclusion for everyone concerned.
I do not question Divine Wisdom in this.
No one and nothing can come between me and my good.
No mistake can harm me for I live and move in God.
No lack of any kind can touch the child of God.
I am that child of God.
The Angel of compassion now surrounds me with her
beautiful light and that light fills my mind
and quenches my thirsting soul.
My heart is opening up to see what God would have me see
in all those whom I have judged or been judged by.
Peace fills the empty chambers of my heart
as I now let go of the past.

From this moment on I choose to look away from
the errors of myself and others.
I choose to learn what God would
have me learn from this
situation now as I let it go.
I choose this day to seek and find the good,
the beautiful and the holy in all God's children.
This relationship is now released to God and
I am happy that it is so.
Thank You Lord for hearing my prayer.
I trust in Your will.
And so it is.
Amen

WEDDING DAY PRAYER

Heavenly Creator, we join with you today
as the dearly beloved of this beautiful couple.
We stand here now as the Holy Witnesses to a most sacred
and holy union as we lift them up to the Light today that
You may pour out Your blessings upon them.
This day is dedicated to a great sacred joining of lives.
As they have been drawn together by love,
may that same love draw us all closer together here and now.
We stand together as a spiritual community to bear
witness to the love & promises given and received.
We commit ourselves now to holding a sacred space in our
hearts and minds for this couple to flourish and grow.
We accept this sacred honor and take seriously our task to
hold the Light for _____ & _____.
Lord, strengthen their love & renew their lives this day
that they may have serious intentions and light hearts.
May their lives blossom and grow in love,
health, abundance and joy.
May all conflicts & differences be quickly resolved & forgiven.

May angels surround and bless their family and home.
May all who know them be blessed by
the presence of such a great love.
Thank You Lord for this new family.
Thank You for this glorious day of celebration.
Amen

PRAYER FOR THE BRIDE

Divine Mother, I am filled with the Light of
radiant love today. Pour out your blessings on me this
day as I pledge myself to a most precious and intimate love
I open my heart now to receive my beloved.
I make a space for him/her to live inside of me.
I take his/her hand this day to walk forward on a
mystical and sacred journey of love.
I now allow my beauty to shine forth as never before.
I do not shrink back from the glory of who
I am on this holy day of joining with my beloved.
This day unfolds effortlessly, joyously and gracefully
according to Divine Will.
There is nothing to worry about, nothing to control -
all is well and God is on the Field.
I relax into the process and let Spirit handle the details.
My light flows forth in all directions and I allow myself to
fully receive all the blessings that are here for us today.
I breathe in the rich splendor of all that I see & feel today.
I am held in the arms of Divine Love today and I extend that
love to all who come to witness this sacred event.
I graciously accept the gift of my beloved today.
I surrender myself gladly to our love.
May this love fill our home and our hearts.
May patience, kindness and joy rule our love.
May my womanhood flower to its fullest strength
and power in the presence of my beloved.
May my beloved grow in gentle patience
and wisdom in my presence.

May Divine Love find a home in us now.
Thank You for this day and for this love.
Amen

PRAYER FOR THE GROOM

Heavenly Father, I am humbled and grateful to have found such a great and glorious love in this world.
I stand joyfully before You today ready to receive this
beautiful gift and ready to surrender myself to its majesty.
I am filled with Grace today.
I breathe in deeply and allow myself to be fully present & alive.
Each breath opens my heart more and more
as it calms my mind and centers me in the now.
I am fully present & I allow the events to unfold before me.
The spirit of Divine Love rules the day.
As I commit myself to this awesome love I allow myself
to drink in the radiance of my beloved as I receive her/him
into my heart to live in joy and appreciation.
I honor the mystery of my beloved.
I make room in my heart and in my life.
I cherish what she/he has brought into my life and I shall
do my best to never be stingy with my compliments or
in showering her/him with my love and gratitude.
I allow myself to grow into my full manhood by honoring
the Divinity that dwells within my beloved.
May we walk together through all things in love & harmony.
May God bless us and our family all the days of our lives.
Thank you Mother-Father God for this miraculous day.
Amen

PRAYER TO CONCEIVE A CHILD

Divine Creator, we open ourselves to receive the gift of a precious child into our hearts.

We make ready now the Consciousness of our home
and open our lives to welcome this new life.
Our bodies, hearts and minds are fertile ground
for the planting of this divine seed within.
From this moment on we treat ourselves and one another
with love, care, patience and nurturing for we know this
is a sacred and holy task we undertake together.
We now call forth some loving little spirit to find a home here.
Relaxing into the Divine Flow of Life we allow the process to
unfold in its own perfect timing and ways.
Lord, if this is the right time, we now open ourselves
to receive this wonderful gift.
May all that we do and say be infused with loving intention.
May we be the parents that You would have us be.
May our lives be a safe haven to guide and protect.
May the love that we have for one another now expand
and multiply in the form of a beloved child.
We surrender this prayer intention to the Universe now.
We trust in the process and in the Divine Wisdom and
Power which turns seeds into flowers, and makes planets
revolve around the sun with no effort or struggle.
Our desires are placed in the One Divine Mind.
Thank You Lord.
Amen

PRAYER TREATMENT FOR HAPPY PREGNANCY & BIRTHING

God, I place myself into in Your hands.
The preciousness of this life within me fills me with
gratitude and I am humbled by the magnitude of this miracle.
I now allow the Divine Wisdom of this process to take over.
I allow myself to be nurtured, helped and supported.
At this very moment Divine Light is filling my body.
Divine Wisdom knows exactly how to run my body and how
to create, nurture and sustain the life within me.
Every moment the Divine Mother within me is giving us all

that we need for a happy & healthy pregnancy.
I now release any fears and relax into this
natural and miraculous process.
My body's changes are welcomed and accepted.
It is okay for me to be emotional & to feel things deeply.
I am beautiful and know that I am taking part
in the precious cycle of life.
My body knows what it needs and I am easily drawn to the
right foods, exercises, books, physicians, and helps as I listen
to and follow my own internal wisdom.
Every hand that touches me is a healing helpful hand.
I am being carried and nurtured by Spirit.
The birth process is witnessed & supported by Angels.
I relax into the process as my baby comes easily, safely and
joyfully into this world and into our hearts.
Angels now surround us and guide this dear
little spirit here to earth at just the right moment.
I accept this blessing with a humble happy heart.
Thank You Lord.
Amen

PRAYER TREATMENT FOR A SICK CHILD

Dear God, I turn to You now that you may shine
Your healing Light on this child I love.
I choose now to hold the Light of healing.
Use me as an instrument of Divine Love – move through me
now to channel comfort and kindness as I pray.
Restore, strengthen and renew the fire of Life - activate full
health and vitality to every cell, organ, tissue and system.
Move through the mind and body to repair & rejuvenate.
Bring forth all the right people and circumstances to help.
Whatever medicine, healing agents or help needed – draw it to
us now and make the way clear as we open to receive.
I know that there is Divine Wisdom in the body that reflects

the perfection of the Holy Healer – I call that Healer forth
now to return the body to its natural state of life abundant.
I release all fears to You now.
I allow myself to hear and follow Your Voice of guidance.
I have consulted the Highest Authority.
I realize that I cannot see or know the ideal path.
I surrender now to Higher Wisdom to guide the way.
Thank You for healing us together.
Amen.

PRAYER BEFORE SURGERY OR MEDICAL PROCEDURE

God, I place myself in Your hands today.
My body and mind belong to You.
I breathe in Your healing love and serenity now and know that
You are healing my mind of all fear and apprehension.
I place Divine Wisdom in charge of this day and this process.
Angels surround me and lift me up.
Unseen Beings of Light guide the hands of everyone associated
in any way with this experience in my life.
Every hand that touches me is a healing helping hand.
Radiant Light flows through my veins and enlivens the cells.
My immune system is activated and balanced by Divine Power.
All medicines taken are infused with the purity of the
Spirit and essence of God's perfect Love.
The past is over and whatever had come
before this moment is forgiven and released.
This is a new day – a new beginning.
I am opening now to allow the forces of healing
to take over my body with Grace and ease.
My mind is focused on calm compassionate breathing.
There is nothing for me to do but relax into the God-flow.
There is nothing to fear – nothing to resist.
All is unfolding now in a state of perfect Grace.
Thank You Lord for taking over.

I let go – I let God.
Amen.

PRAYER FOR MY HOME

Divine Love fills and surrounds my home.
I am safe here for I am sheltered by the love of God.
My home and all my surroundings are beautiful and
supportive to my own inner-awareness of the comfort
and beauty of the Spirit behind all things.
This is a warm and inviting environment for
myself and all those who enter.
There is always more than enough money to
pay the bills and to sustain my home with all
that I need in order to live joyfully and abundantly.
This is a sacred place and I fill it with the God-vibration
which attracts wonderful people and experiences.
This is a refuge and a sanctuary.
I find my rest here.
The rooms are filled with the laughter of those I love.
This is the background for many wonderful
memories yet to come.
My home reflects the highest and best within me and
is a constant reminder that I am an able,
capable and loving person.
The neighborhood in which I live is a loving, safe place.
I love and bless my neighbors and send this blessing out
my front door and into the streets of this town.
There are Angels at the door, on the street corners
and in every home I see.
All darkness is banished and Divine Light protects us all.
There is nothing to fear.
I allow myself to belong here.
I allow myself to have this blessing.
Thank You God that it is so.
Amen

ENTERING THE TEMPLE

I know that I am safe in God's loving care.
I let go of all concepts I have about myself.
I lay aside my past and future goals.
I rid myself of all mistakes, grievances and faults.
I release what think I want or need in order to be happy.
I unburden myself as I breathe in the cool and gentle air.
It is safe for me to relax and let go for I am in the Temple;
the Secret Place of the Most High.
I am bathed in the glow of a thousand candles.
Angels sing to me songs of peace and love beyond measure.
My heart softens in the love which floods my being.
I am in His presence now and I am safe.
Here, I seek and find the forgiveness that I need.
I turn away from the outer world and
all that concerns me there.
Here I am safe to be who I really am.
There is nothing to get and nothing to want.
I am in the presence of all the saints and prophets.
Jesus, Moses, Mary and the Buddha live here,
and I abide with them.
I am washed clean in the living waters.
I am anointed by the Angels.
My spirit is renewed and I am filled with vital energy.
The life force within me grows strong.
My burdens have been lifted from me and
I am able to return to the world with a heart
full of compassion and serenity.
Thank You Lord that this is so.
Amen

PRAYER FOR OUR PETS

There is a Divinity in all animals everywhere & all of the animals of the world are blessed by an angel of God.
I place my pets in the care of that angel now.
Divine love now enfolds my animal friends and
keeps them safe from all sickness and harm.
I send out my love and appreciation now for their
companionship and unwavering love.
There is an unbroken bond of communication between us
which supports us both in knowing that we are not alone.
My heart is overflowing.
This is a sacred trust and I gladly accept the
responsibility of this precious and tender life.
I make time for my pet and lovingly groom and care
for him with tenderness and loving-kindness.
I know that right now the consciousness of all
human-kind is shifting to honor the Divinity in all of life,
including these precious creatures.
The world is being transformed into a safe habitat for animals
to live with us in safety, harmony and balance.
We are all able to thrive in the light of God's love.
I devote myself now to not only knowing the truth
of this but also to doing whatever I can to be a human who is
responsible for living in harmony with nature.
I place the animals in the care of God.
May I do no harm.
May I be of help.
Thank You God.
Amen

Prayer for The Loss Of A Loved One

I open my heart now that I may be healed.
I allow myself to feel the deep emotions which
fill my being and I know that I am not alone in my pain.
There is an angel of mercy and compassion
who is beside me now.
It is safe for me to grieve and I know that I am comforted by
the love of God which surrounds me.
There is no loss except in time and I realize that in
the reality of Spirit I am still one with this person.
Divine comfort fills me and heals my wounded heart.
The grace of God is running my life while I am in mourning.
There is nothing to resist nor rush through for I honor this
sacred cycle of birth, death and rebirth.
All is well in the Universe and I am forever part of all that is.
I let go of our physical relationship and give
thanks that we had this time together on Earth.
I now open up to a relationship of the spirit.
I release this person to their greater and highest good now
as I focus on the essence of our love for one another.
All communication is now heart-communication.
There is no space nor distance in the heart.
I know that my loved one lives on
inside me and we are together.
This day I seek and find the comfort of the Divine Mother.
May I be held in the Divine arms.
May I be cradled by the angels.
I rest in God.
May my loved one rest in God as well.
I let go.
I let God.
Thank You Lord.
Amen

PRAYER FOR VETERANS AND SOLDIERS

Blessings on the men and women who have
stood up for their country and for their beliefs.
This very day the angels of justice and mercy surround each
one of them and bathe them in a divine protective light.
Peace reigns down this day from Heaven.
All is well and every man, woman and child may live in serenity
knowing that God is holding the world in His hands.
All those who have been injured or harmed in any way
by the tragedy of war are this very moment
being healed by Divine Restoration.
All that they need is drawn to them now.
Love, friendship, prosperity, acknowledgment, assistance and
health are their Divine Inheritance this very day.
All obstacles to peace and plenty dissolve
in the blaze of God's fiery love.
All minds are healed, bodies cared for and hearts mended.
The Holy Spirit now takes every memory of pain and darkness
and cuts the cords which bound them to the mind.
Sweet relief is breathed in and all is well.
Praise God for these brave and noble ones who
followed their inner-call.
May they be safe from all harm.
May they recover quickly from
any and all illness, disease or injury.
May there never be another moment of
fighting, violence or injustice on the Earth.
May any need for armies end.
May we learn to love and honor one another.
I now join my thoughts to the Holiest of Holies
that my mind may be cleansed of all anger,
resentment and violence.
May peace begin with me. May it begin now.
Please help us God. Thank You Lord.
Amen

BODY/FOOD PRAYER

God is everywhere present and can heal all things.
The Holy Spirit is healing my mind of all judgment
and pain regarding my body and food.
I release any guilt, shame or hopelessness over my body.
I now choose to have healthy and loving
relationships with my body, exercise and food.
I love, bless and accept my body regardless
of its appearance, shape or size and
I am so grateful to it for it serving me so well.
I do not use my body to store emotions
nor do I use food to comfort me or ease my pain.
Spirit now harmonizes, balances and restores every cell of my
body as well as my physical, emotional and mental appetites.
I enjoy healthy nutritious foods and
release all guilt regarding eating.
I bless everything that I eat and never curse my food.
I speak only loving words about food & my body.
I let Spirit within guide me to making the best
food choices for my particular body today.
I invite Jesus to eat with me and to remove all
guilt as I eat with joy the foods that we choose together
This body is a holy expression of Consciousness in form.
I treat it with loving-kindness and deep respect.
It is unique and there is no outer ideal
for me to ever compare myself with.
My body finds its perfect balance and weight.
There is nothing to change, fix or manipulate.
There is no need for rigid control, discipline or deprivation.
My appetite is wholesome and regulated by Spirit.
I do not deserve to be punished in any way.
I am at peace with myself and my sexuality.
It is safe for me to be physically attractive and beautiful.
There is nothing to fear.
I am worthy and beautiful and all is well.
I embrace my sensuality and I do not use my body to "get"

anything nor to keep anything or anyone away.
The past is over and no one can hurt, abuse nor
violate me in any way. I accept only respectful love.
I now love and accept my body for the
divine and precious gift that it is.
May it be used by Spirit to do God's will.
It is forgiven and I am forgiven and we are released together.
I allow myself to have a beautiful, healthy,
strong and attractive body.
Praise God for this miraculous healing.
Thank You Jesus for walking with me today.
I am filled with love. And so it is.
Amen

BLESSING BEFORE A MEAL

In gratitude and joy we sit in the presence of the Divine
as we join together to celebrate this meal.
This food is blessed by the spirits of love and abundance
to nourish our bodies and strengthen us to live with vitality.
We are thankful for this chance to come together as family
and friends to acknowledge that which is sacred in
the ritual of taking in sustenance.
May we grow in love here today.
May we open to hear one another.
May our conversation be meaningful and intimate.
May joy find place at this table.
May our hearts be light.
May all feel welcome and at home.
Join with us now Lord as we acknowledge
Your Presence here with us.
Thank You for another day together.
Thank You for this life.
Amen

Prayer for Safe Travel

As I take this journey I send out my loving thoughts before me to light up the way with happy loving experiences.
There is no time nor place where I can be separate from God
and I am on safe and holy ground wherever I go.
All stress, worry and anxiety dissolve as I relax and let go.
My travel is safe and comfortable.
Planes, trains, cars, buses and boats are all the same to God
and I now invite Him to take the helm and lead the way.
My accommodations fill my every need are just right for me.
The entire Universe is my home for God is with me always.
No one is a stranger to me but only a brother or sister
I have yet to embrace.
My Divine Companion travels with me this day and
I am guided through all things by this Guardian Angel.
The spirit of joy is spread out before me like a carpet that
welcomes me everywhere I go.
I am surrounded by congenial loving people and my way is
made easy and straight. All is well.
All that is necessary to have a successful and happy trip
is drawn to me by Divine Attraction.
My days are filled with Divine Activity.
There is no need to worry or rush.
I am on God's schedule and all my experiences unfold
according to Divine Timing. I relax into this truth.
I open my heart and mind to experience
the goodness that is all around me.
I let go of control and allow God to
take care of every need I may have.
No harm can come to me nor my companions for the Divine
Mother has her loving arms around us now.
I am so grateful for this opportunity to see
what God would have me see and to
meet those whom God would have me meet.
I embrace the perfection of this glorious and holy day.
I am at home.

I am peaceful and happy.
Thank You God.
Amen

PRAYER FOR FINANCIAL ABUNDANCE

There is no lack in God and none in me.
As the Universe is infinite & knows no limits, neither do I.
I am one with all of Life and that Creative Principle of Life
creates abundance through and for me.
There is no need to hoard nor squander.
I constantly attract financial prosperity
and I am a grateful receiver.
I always have more than enough money to pay my bills, enjoy
my life and to contribute and share my wealth
with those I love as Spirit directs.
I am not afraid of prosperity and I relinquish all my
judgments about money and about wealthy people.
I know that it is God's will that all His children be provided for
in every way possible and I will not oppose His will with
thoughts or beliefs about struggle and poverty.
Abundance is the most natural law of the world for there are
more than enough grains of sand on the beach, stars in the sky
and the Universe is forever expanding and making more.
I let go of all past patterns and beliefs about money.
I forgive my parents for any fears I may have learned from
them regarding money and prosperity.
My mind is now healed.
I allow myself to receive my good now for
I am a trustworthy steward with money and
know that money is merely a form of energy.
There is nothing good nor bad about money and prosperity -
abundance is as natural as breathing in and breathing out.
I allow myself to enjoy saving, spending, investing, tithing,
circulating and playing with money.

I use money lovingly and joyfully.
I follow the Holy Spirit's inner direction as to what to do with
all my finances for I realize that God is the Source of my
supply regardless of the particular human vessels which
He uses to distribute the flow.
Thank You Lord for trusting me with this wonderful supply.
May I do only good with it. May it bless the world.
Money is a good friend who comes to play happy games
and I am ready to play in the most joyous ways today.
So it is and so I let it be.
Amen

PRAYER FOR RELEASE FROM FEAR & ANXIETY

D ear Lord, I admit that I am afraid and I know that
You are not the author of fear.
From this moment on I let go of
terrorizing myself with my thoughts.
Today I will not condone nor indulge
my own worrying and obsessive negativity.
Today I believe Your hand is upon my shoulders leading and
guiding me through all situations and controlling all outcomes.
I realize I am not alone and I have a Companion Who knows
who I am and what I need. Divine Aid is mine now.
I take a deep breath and surrender all my fears
into the arms of the Divine Mother.
Nothing and no one can interfere with the miracles I now
claim for myself and for this situation.
All anxiety, dread and panic dissolve now and
I allow my body to relax and let go.
My shoulders drop, my jaw and forehead relax and all
tension is released into the White Light of Your Divine Love.
My heart is beginning to soften as
I release being right about my fears.
I am an innocent child of God who believes in the

miracles which defy all the laws of this world.
I surrender now into the laws of God.
I will not project my thoughts into the future.
I will not keep repeating my past. My faith is in You God.
I know that You are greater than
any person, condition or situation.
I am washed clean in the Living Waters.
It is easy for me to breathe in and breathe out for the Holy
Spirit now enters my body and clears my mind of all thoughts
which do not bring peace, clarity and calm.
Thank You Lord for the answer to all my problems.
Thank You for walking with me today.
I love You and trust You in all things and in all ways.
Amen

PRAYER FOR HEALING NEGATIVITY

Lord, I know that my own cleverness
has been used against me at times.
My intelligence and insights have sometimes brought me pain.
I confess that my past hurts have sometimes hardened me
against love and increased my emotional armor.
This is not how I want to live.
I now let down these defenses.

I let go of being right and quick and clever.
I let go of my observations of what and who is wrong.
I release my cynicism and doubts.
I am now filled with Your holy innocence.
It is safe for me to trust in Your love and protection.
It is safe for me to relax and let go.
I choose from this day on to forgive quickly.
I will no longer do mental reruns of past hurts.
I now choose to think of the Universe as a friendly place.
I choose to notice the good in people and in situations.

I seek a new mind and a new heart.
From this moment on Divine thinking fills my world.
I am attracted to and notice the good all around me.
I am part of that good which lights the Universe.
I now realize that all things are unfolding perfectly for my
highest and best good and I welcome this new life.
I am given another chance to live joyfully.
I offer this new self to You God.
Heal me now Father.
Bless me Divine Mother.
Give me wings to fly that my heart may soar.
Amen

PRAYER FOR HEALING A BROKEN HEART

God, the pain I now feel is deep and it's burden is great.
I keep repeating my thoughts of the past and what has
happened over and over.
Please heal my mind of the tendency to dwell in the past.
Heal my heart of this aching wound.
I know that Your angel of mercy is here beside me now and
I lean on the heavenly shoulder for comfort.
Whatever tears are left are cleansing me and
I allow myself to cry them all.
I allow myself now to move through this process
so that I may be reborn.
I will heal from this and I will love again with Your help.
I am willing to let go of the past as best I can.
May only the blessing of our love remain.
I will not use this as a reason to harden myself
nor to withdraw from life.
I deserve love and happiness.
I know that it is God's will for me.
I release this person now to their highest and best good.
I know that as I release my partner, I am released as well.

I cannot move on while holding onto grievances or to the past.
From this moment on I shall increase in love and strength.
My heart is healing and opening up
to experience what is next for me.
There is no delay in God's plan for my life and for my good.
I gratefully allow myself to be guided
and led by the Holy Spirit.
Even now the seeds of love are
planted and rooted in my heart.
My eyes are opening up to see the
new opportunities that are here and now.
I am drawn to that which is for my highest good.
Unseen angels guide my every step,
my every thought, my every action.
Nothing good is withheld from me and I know
that I deserve to be well-loved in this life.
Thank You Divine Spirit for this miraculous healing.
I give myself to You.
Amen.

Prayer for Healing Loneliness & Isolation

Oh Lord, for too long I have punished and
denied myself with this isolation.
I hid myself away from the world and thought I was safe.
I realize that I only hurt myself more by cutting myself
off from the loving company of other people.
I realize that I am never truly alone for
You are here beside me.
And now I seek Your presence in the hearts
of my brothers and sisters here on Earth.
I now breathe Your loving presence into
the silent chambers of my heart.
I fill the emptiness with my Divine Companion.
There is no lack of people in the world and I now allow my

heart to fill with love for all people everywhere.
I am surrounded by the goodness of humankind.
I let go of thoughts that I am not good enough.
I let go of my judgmental thoughts of others.
Right now Divine Spirit is drawing to me
wonderful loving friends & experiences.
The Universe knows who are the ideal companions
for me and now draws us together.
We find joy in one another's company.
We share life's journey and walk the path together.
We open our heart's to one another's differences
and accept the gift of learning from them.
Thank You Divine Mother and Father that
I live in a world filled with limitless possibilities
and potential for harmonious relationships.
I open myself now to let people in.
It is safe for me to love and be loved.
I release all unconscious hurts and resistance to people now
and I allow myself to reach out to other people.
I am no longer afraid of revealing myself.
Serenity, confidence and peace fill me as I now approach the
people who are put in my pathway - I reach out my hand now
and greet them with love and friendship.
I am a worthwhile person and I deserve
to have a life filled with loving companions.
I will do my best to not decide where these people shall come
from, what they should look like, what their background or
goals should be - I instead, place my faith in Your deciding for
me who and where we shall meet on this joyous path of Light.
In love and gratitude and praise I release this to
the perfect unfolding by effortless grace as
I follow the Guidance and opportunities that open up to me
Thank You Mother-Father God.
Amen

PRAYER BEFORE A DATE

Dear God, I surrender all my thoughts about
this date and about this person to You.
I let go of projecting my goals and needs onto
this person so that I may see who they truly are.
My best self now comes forward and
I stand strong in Divine Confidence.
There is no need for me to be anything other than my real self.
I relax into being exactly who I am and who I am not.
I let go of trying to please, impress or gain approval.
I focus on the joy of getting to know this person
and sharing myself with them.
I open my heart to seeing who this person really is.
I let go of my judgments.
I release my past experiences of dating
and relationships and am healed.
I let go of any blockages, negative thoughts or cynical nature.
I let go of feeling I am not good enough.
I let go of thinking that others are not good enough.
I know that I am a precious gift of God
in whom He is well pleased.
I release all fear. My heart is at peace now. All is well.
Peace and joy are my only goals.
There is nothing to strive for nor to "get".
I do not go on this date alone, but walk with the Holy Spirit.
I call my real self forward now and I relax into this experience.
This is an experience of joy and sharing of two souls.
I speak from my heart with no hidden agendas or goals.
It is safe for me to show up fully
and to let my light shine freely.
I am already filled with God's love and
I share this light with all whom are near me.
Nothing and no one can ever diminish my inner-light.
Lord, walk with us now so that no matter what
the outcome we will feel happy and at peace.
All now unfolds beautifully and easily according to Your will.

Thank You for this wonderful experience.
May we both be blessed.
Amen

PREPARATION PRAYER FOR SEX

L ord, I surrender this most beautiful act to the living spirit
of love which radiates through all life.
This sharing with my partner is an act
of spirit moving through the flesh.
I let go of any feelings of guilt or false beliefs regarding sex.
I fully move into my body and I celebrate
and share its beauty and the beauty of my partner.
I let go of my critical mind and judgments
that I may be fully present in my heart.
I allow myself to be open and vulnerable to this person.
I release my thoughts of all past sexual experiences so
that I may fully enjoy whatever unexpected
pleasures come from the present moment.
I let go of any predetermined outcome or goal and
relax into the sharing of physical intimacy with my partner.
May this be a blending of physical, spiritual and
mental desires to give and receive pleasure and love.
May this experience be a greater joining of two souls
and not a way to hide from one another.
May it reflect our inner-selves.
May we deeply surrender to one another.
May we grow closer in love and communication.
May our love come shining through.
Thank You Divine Father Mother for joining with us now.
Amen

PRAYER FOR FAMILY HEALING

Dear God, I place my family in Your hands now.
These people are so dear and precious to my heart and
yet there are ways in which we have hurt
and disappointed one another.
Misunderstandings and fear have built up walls that have kept
our love from coming through as brilliantly as we meant it to.
There are times when we have strayed far from
our hearts and spoken from our pain.
We have attacked and defended and left one another scarred.
Please take all of this past hurt away now.
Bring to the forefront the love that has always been there.
I know that all life is forever bound together in
the Divine and Holy consciousness of God.
My family and I are part of that Divine Mind.
Come into us now.
I now surrender my own wounds from the past and
am willing to see everyone in a completely new way.
Restore my mind now to Eternal Truth.
I will not look on the mistakes and guilt of those around me.
I will no longer hold onto my own mistakes or lovelessness.
I forgive myself and I forgive my family.
The past is over and has no power over me.
I feel the loving eyes of God upon us.
I now claim for myself and for this family
a radical healing of the heart and mind.
From this moment on the Angels will lift us
to the very highest places in our minds.
Nothing can delay the will of God and
I know that Your will is our happiness.
We are restored in this Holy Instant of forgiveness.
I breathe in this truth. I place my faith in the Lord.
Thank You Divine Mother.
Praise the Divine Father.
And so it is. Amen

PRAYER FOR EMPOWERED AGING

Dear God, I thank You for bringing me to this place in my life. So many of my companions did not make it this far and I sometimes fear that one day I will
stand all alone in this world.
I release these fears to You now.
I am at peace with my past and honor the people
and the path that brought me here today.
I am an ageless spirit and I embrace
the wisdom of my life experiences.
I bless this body which I inhabit and
fill it with the Holy Breath of Life.
Each breath I take renews and restores the cells
of my body and dissolves all worry and pain.
My mind is clear and sharp and I am
interested in the life all around me.
I release my body and mind from the past
and from any effects of past hurts.
I am forever an effect of the Divine Ageless
Spirit of Wisdom and Love eternal.
All that remains of my past experience are
the lessons of love given and received.
I harbor no resentments or anger against anyone or anything.
My life begins anew each and every morning.
It is never too late for me to begin anything
for I live by the God-clock.
I am forever in the right place at the right time.
Today is the day - this is the moment.
I am enthusiastic about exactly where I am at this point in my
life and I do not allow the voices of the world to tell me
who I am or what my place is.
I have a purpose that only grows stronger and more
magnificent with each year.
All those who for whom a relationship with me is mutually
beneficial are irresistibly drawn to my side now.
It is never too late for me to form loving new relationships.

My body and mind know no age.
My face and my body are lit from within by a full
and rich life of love and learning.
I stand here in Your Presence and look out
onto the horizon at all the adventures yet to come.
My best years are still ahead of me!
I walk in Your Light.
Your Love enfolds me.
This body is blessed to serve me well.
I have so much yet to give and to experience.
Make joyful use of me Lord.
I am ready for fabulous new adventures.
Amen

PRAYER FOR HEALING MELANCHOLY

Lord, I have allowed my thoughts to sink into darkness.
I have bound and trapped myself in a cycle of
hopelessness and pain. This is not where I want to be.
I want to feel Your joy in me and in my life.
I want so much to feel myself wrapped in Your Divine Arms.
Come into me now. Heal me and fill me with Your Light.
I gladly release the thoughts and feelings which have
haunted me and driven me to this place.
I do not want these old thoughts & beliefs anymore and
I gently and firmly release them from my mind and heart.
All fear is now vanquished and dissipates into the Light.
From this moment on I claim for myself
abundant life and renewed interest in living.
Whatever thoughts or experiences have brought me into the
dark night - I dissolve them now.
They have no power over me for I stand in Divine Light.
Nothing can touch me or deter me from my right path.
By the power of my word I now claim
the joy and happiness that God has willed to me.

Let nothing and no one come between me and my inner-light.
This is my new beginning Lord.
Thank You for this healing.
Thank You for this moment in time.
I love you and I am learning now to love myself.
Praise God now.
Amen

PRAYER FOR DEALING WITH REJECTION

Lord, I feel defeated and discouraged.
I put myself out there and it seems that the result
was hurtful to me and to my sense of self.
In a moment of vulnerability my tender self
was somehow squelched. But that is not who I am.
In spite of this hurt, I know that these feelings
are not the truth about me.
The truth about me is grander and
greater than any single experience.
The truth about me is greater than
the approval or acceptance of others.
I will resist the temptation to harbor negativity about
myself or toward those whom I feel did not want my gift.
I know that there is a reason for everything
that occurs in me and in my world and
I accept that this is for my best and highest good.
Another door is opening for me even now.
There are limitless opportunities for my good
and I invoke them now.
My eyes are opening to new possibilities and
I am renewed and strengthened by Divine Spirit.
I know that right now those whom
will love and appreciate who and what I am are on
their way to me and I release all past experience in
order to stand ready for the new.

I acknowledge myself for having shown up
for life and for participating.
I respect and honor myself for taking the chance.
Thank You for the opportunity to play in the game of life.
I open my heart to learn whatever You
would have me learn from this situation.
I will not use it as a block to my own growth nor
as an excuse to play small in the future.
I am the same one I always was and nothing
can change my beauty and brilliance.
I was created by You just as I am.
I bless and release all participants in this situation to their
greater good and I bless myself for my courage and willingness.
I am lovable, capable and worthy.
Praise God for all that I have been given.
Amen

PRAYER FOR ANOTHER PERSON

Dear Lord, I place the life of _____,
into Your loving and powerful hands.
I know that Your love is filling and surrounding him/her now.
In this moment I claim for _____ a Divine
Intervention and Healing of all circumstances and
I know that my prayer is heard.
I release my will and place this person into Your hands now.
I declare now that _____'s every need is taken care
of in this moment and that his/her Divine Inheritance is
fulfilled and effortlessly sustained and maintained.
May the Angels surround and lift _____ up.
May there be an end of pain and a return of
joy and peace and laughter.
May all sorrows be comforted and lifted.
May I be of help in whatever way You guide me to be.
Right now in this very moment every cell of

_____'s body is being infused with
the Healing Light of Christ.
Every breath comes easily and restores,
soothes, energizes and heals.
They feel this love now.
Any and all sickness, disease or despair
vanishes in this Holy Instant.
All poverty, lack and emotional turmoil cease.
Anger is released - resentments dissipate.
The Holy Mother cradles _____ in Her arms.
The power of the love in my heart gives wings to this prayer
and delivers the healing now.
Nothing can deny the will of God. All is well .I release this
into Divine Hands and trust that all outcomes are right.
And so it is. And so I let it be.
Amen

Prayer for Healing Addictions

Dear Lord, I feel so out of control and insane.
I do not know who I am anymore and it feels as if
I have lost my way back to a safe harbor.
I sometimes feel guilty and ashamed and yet I know that
You have not turned Your face from me.
I want so much to be released from this bondage.
I want to live again and to be free at last.
I need to feel Your forgiveness wash over me -
to cleanse me of this illness, of this despair and longing.
I claim a miracle for myself now.
I claim my Divine Inheritance.
I know that I am still Your child and that Your power is
flowing through my body and mind even now.
I am being restored by the power of Your grace.
I am not alone.
I am no longer lost.
I am being healed by Divine Love.
My life begins anew and the past is washed away.

My desires are now transformed and I want only what is
wholesome, helpful and right for me.
I am allowing myself to be relaxed and at peace inside.
God has heard my call.
I am safe at last from all harm and unhealthy desires.
I give thanks now that I am being healed and made whole
and I release this process to Spirit as I learn to make
good choices and to keep going in the right direction.
Thank You Great Spirit for guiding me now.
Amen

HOLIDAY PRAYER

Dear God, I surrender all my thoughts
and expectations about this holy season to You.
I release myself and my loved ones from my own agenda and
goals so that we may more fully embrace what You would have
us experience.
May we all be blessed by a greater experience of mindfulness,
serenity and love.
I now choose to remember what is truly important.
There is no need to rush, hurry or to do everything exactly
right - I am enough just as I am.
Gifts, cooking, decorating, cards and parties are wonderful but
merely surface manifestations of an inner-experience.
Let me not forget this.
It is okay for things to be messier than usual.
It is okay if I do not get everything done.
The perfection of this season is not in outer things, but rather
in the Light that is within me now.
May my heart open wide to all the miracles that are unfolding
in my life this very moment.
May I see the angels that surround me.
May I be an angel for someone else.
Thank You Lord. Amen

NEW YEAR PRAYER

Dear Lord, I stand here at the threshold of a new year.
The past is fading behind, the future is still
a bright light just ahead, full of joyful promise.
I take a moment now to breathe in the Holy Present.
Stand with me now - be the Guide Who
clears my mind and opens my heart.
I gently and gratefully release the year past.
I bless it all: the good and the bad, the pain
and the joy, the teachers and the lessons learned.
It is over now and only the love remains.
The year before me is yet a blank page -
Write Your name on it Dear Lord.
Fill each day with your Holy Presence.
Make me a child of Light.
This is who I am.
This is why I came.
My mind is filled with Holy Spirit Power.
The road is set before me.
The path made straight.
From this moment on I shall never walk alone.
Praise God for this new year, this new day.
Amen

The

Exercises

and

Favorite

Teachings

Jacob Glass

THE FOUR PROBLEMS AND ANSWERS

On spiritual path does not make us immune to problems and issues arising. But it's good to know just what kind of problem it is so that we can use our spiritual toolbox to do our work properly. Our issues tend to be one of 4 areas. Here are the questions to help guide us through the process – whether we need to turn up the love, clean up our thinking, surrender to Grace, or take some action.

Is this a Love issue?

- *Do I need to forgive myself or another?* WE MUST LET GO OF GRIEVANCES
- *Am I closing my heart off?* WE MUST HAVE AN OPEN HEART/OPEN VALVE TO RECEIVE
- *Am I indulging in attack thoughts?* LOVE THINKS KINDLY, IS NOT EASILY ANGERED
- *Am I being defensive in order to protect my heart/feelings?* MUST BE VULNERABLE IN LOVE
- *Am I busy strategizing rather than being present?* SLOW DOWN TO THE SPEED OF LOVE
- *Am I withholding love and/or approval from someone close to me or myself?* GIVE
- *Am I not being loving to myself and thinking in terms of win-lose rather than win-win?* WIN-WIN OR NO DEAL
- *Am I coming from kindness and walking in Love?*

Is this a Mental Law issue?

- *Am I being sloppy in my thinking and speaking?*
- *Am I not taking responsibility for what I focus on and am doing with my energy and Consciousness?*
- *Have I fallen back into limited fearful thinking and old negative mental habits?*

78

- *Am I defending my limitations? Am I calling limited thinking "facts?"*
- *Am I hanging out in "hope" and superstitious religious thinking or waiting for someone to save me?*
- *Am I being wishy-washy, not making decisions, not asking for what I want and/or playing helpless victim?*

Is this a Grace issue?

- *Am I thinking I know what is best for myself and everyone else – that I have the answer and need things to turn out a certain way in order for me to be happy?*
- *If I am doing MY part and yet I am feeling frustrated, impatient, tormented, etc. – even though I have done my part of the Love walk and have done my Mental Law work, then it's definitely time to come from non-attachment and SURRENDER fully to Grace.*
- *Have I TRULY consulted a Higher Authority?*

Is this an Action issue?

- *Knowing the problem and the answer is not the same thing as ACTIVATING the answer through doing the work. Knowing about the gym is different than going and actually working out there. Am I not DOING what I KNOW to do?*
- *Am I being CONSISTENT, or are my efforts sporadic? Our lives are most changed by THINGS WE DO EVERY DAY, not by things we do once in a while.*
- *Grace is about SURRENDER to the Holy Spirit*

AFFIRMATIONS AND SPIRITUAL REMINDERS:

I open myself to this new day-
I do not know what is going to happen and so
I allow Divine Spirit to unfold all things perfectly.

I always have what I need.

Lots can happen!

Divine Activity fills my day and runs my life.

Today I remember to praise and acknowledge
the people in my life. I am a grateful child of God today.

My body is strong, healthy and fit.

The good that I seek is now seeking me.

Thank You God for manifesting the perfect
outcome in every area of my life.

I am available for miracles

I am healed by the love I give.

This is an abundant universe and
I am open to receive my good.

I am an instrument of Divine Love and Healing.

I am a beautiful person inside and out.

I love myself fully and freely today.

I allow myself to love all people today.

I am always in the right place at the right time.

I am surrounded and filled with the grace of God.

MY AFFIRMATIONS AND SPIRITUAL REMINDERS

This page is for writing your own affirmations and spiritual reminders

_____

_____

_____

_____

_____

_____

_____

_____

_____

_____

_____

_____

_____

_____

_____

_____

_____

_____

_____

_____

_____

_____

_____

_____

_____

_____

_____

_____

THE MIND HEALING PROCESS

HEALING THE MIND is not a matter of thinking only positive thoughts (as if that were even possible). We all have negative thoughts - but we don't have to set the table and invite them to dinner. When disturbed by a thought, stop and ask yourself, *"Is this thought high enough for the child of God?"* If it's not, then release it from your mind and send it back to the nothingness from whence it came. Try the process below when you recognize that your thoughts are not bringing you peace.

QUESTIONS FOR THE HEALING PROCESS:

- *Is this thought the real, honest truth and do I want to continue to hold onto it and be right about it?*

- *Who am I not forgiving?*

- *What does my judgment cost me?*

- *Is this thought one that I really want to believe?*

- *How does this thought make me feel?*

- *What's my payoff in feeling this way?*

- *Do I want to continue to feel this way?*

- *Would I rather be right or happy?*

- *How do I want to feel?*

- *What is the highest most loving thought that I could think that would help me feel the way I want?*

AGREEMENTS FOR SUCCESSFUL LIVING

I take 100% responsibility for my own life, happiness, healing and what I get out of each day and every experience. I do not expect others to fix me or make me happy.

I agree to love myself <u>no matter what</u>!

I agree to do whatever it takes to stay centered and clear.

I take responsibility for communicating my feelings appropriately and I agree to communicate when something is not working for me.

I commit to daily spiritual renewal through conscious contact with God in whatever way works best for me.

I do not have to communicate if doing so is unsafe or would harm myself or another. I seek divine guidance regarding appropriateness.

I will express my love and gratitude to those around me whenever I can.

I agree to ask for help when I need it. I let go of expecting people to read my mind or know what I want and need.

I release my loved ones from my expectations that they will meet those wants and needs once I have communicated them.

I agree to communicate my feelings as best I can without attack or blame.

I will help others as best I can without taking responsibility for their lives, happiness or experiences.

I release others from participating in my self-destructive patterns and I release myself from participating in the self-destructive patterns of others.

I agree to keep a positive mental attitude and I agree to learn with joy and to trust the process.

I will learn to say no without feeling guilty.

HAPPINESS BOOT CAMP

The Happiness Boot Camp is a 30 day program to kickstart your emotional journey to joy, peace and a positive vibrational shift. I realize it's a lot to do and that it's challenging – but if it were easy it wouldn't be boot camp.

- 30 DAY FAST FROM **ALL** NEWS: TV, INTERNET, NEWSPAPERS AND RADIO. THIS IS THE DETOX.
- READ *"ASK AND IT IS GIVEN"* BY ESTHER HICKS – particularly during any time when you would ordinarily be reading, listening to or watching the news. Try some of the 21 exercises from the book.
- **MORNING** JOURNAL LISTS: MUST BE DONE DAILY! THIS IS THE **MOST** IMPORTANT PART OF BOOT CAMP.
    1. GRATITUDE/APPRECIATION LIST: LIST 10
    2. WHERE *I* GOT IT RIGHT/ACKNOWLEDGE SELF: LIST AT LEAST 9 FROM PREVIOUS 24 HOURS.
    3. WHAT WENT RIGHT: LIST 10 FROM YESTERDAY
    4. "THE DAY I CHOOSE" LIST: ANY # FOR TODAY
- ELIMINATE **ALL** OF THE 4 EMOTIONAL CANCERS:
    1. CRITICIZING
    2. COMPLAINING
    3. COMPETING
    4. COMPARING
- USE THE EMOTIONAL CANCER "NEUTRALIZERS" TO REPLACE THE OLD HABITS:
    1. Criticizing becomes CREATING what YOU want and letting go of what others are up to.
    2. Complaining becomes CHOOSING how YOU will respond or what positive action you will take.
    3. Competing becomes COOPERATING or Partnering with the Universe and others.
    4. Comparing becomes CLAIMING your own life path and COMPLIMENTING yourself for the wonderful unique way that YOU are choosing to live now.

- A BRISK 20 MINUTE WALK EVERY DAY – OUTSIDE IF AT ALL POSSIBLE.
- GET AT LEAST ONE MASSAGE IF POSSIBLE THIS MONTH
- GIVE ONE <u>ANONYMOUS</u> GIFT EACH WEEK
- CLEAN UP ONE MESS IN YOUR LIFE THAT YOU'VE BEEN AVOIDING: TAXES, THE GARAGE, A COMMUNICATION – TAKE PENGUIN STEPS TO MAKE IT DO-ABLE. ASK FOR SUPPORT OR HELP FROM SOMEONE IF NECESSARY.
- IF YOU HAVE TROUBLING THOUGHTS THAT YOU CANNOT SHAKE, WHETHER ABOUT OTHERS OR SELF, DO *"THE WORK"* OF BYRON KATIE. WWW.THEWORK.COM
- DO AT LEAST WEEKLY LISTS OF THE "POSITIVE ASPECTS" OF 3 PEOPLE CLOSE TO YOU – list 10 things each: could be a mate, roommate, co-worker, friend – even (perhaps particularly) those you have problems with.

WHEN ANYTHING THREATENS YOUR PEACE REMEMBER THIS: THE QUESTION IS NOT *"Why did this happen? The bigger question is, What will I make of this now that it has happened?"* TAKE BACK YOUR POWER TO PERCEIVE FOR YOURSELF.

FAVORITE JACOB TEACHINGS

OVER THESE MANY YEARS of teaching there are some things that I tend to say over and over again in my classes, lectures and writings. I am including some of them here for those who find them helpful to have as little nuggets for quick reference.

––––––––––––––––

To the ego life is usually about limitation and finite options – *"I'll either get this job or we'll lose the house and be out on the street!"* To Spirit, all things are possible and we do not have to know the answer. Our job is to open up to the Infinite. One favorite way to do this is to simply affirm, *"Lots can happen!"* To Source there may be limitless options and we do not have to know what they are. We simply invoke them by relaxing into the awareness that lots can happen.

Do not let the ego steal your joy.

No one can give you what you are unwilling to give yourself. The Universe is a mirror. It reflects. If we give to ourselves, we will attract others who will also give to us. If we withhold from ourselves, we will attract others who will also withhold from us.

Learn to EXPECT good every day instead of expecting a struggle. We prepare for what we expect, and what we prepare for we are activating within us. ACTIVATE THE GOOD by expecting good.

Rather than believing in something, believe it in. Robert Frost said, *"Our founding fathers did not believe in the future, they believed it in."*

The desire to be special is a form of depressing insanity. I live in Hollywood, a place where being gorgeous, brilliant and talented is commonplace - but it is also a place of tremendous suffering and dissatisfaction. Being special is the booby prize of life. I'm as common and ordinary as dirt, but many people have said that I'm the happiest person they know. I am happy to the extent that I've given up the idea of being special. To me, "special" is code for tormented. The sunrise and sunset put zero effort into being special. No flower is making an effort to be noticed. The rainbow is being an ordinary average everyday rainbow. But calling a human being "average" is a horrific insult in the world that we live in. It's a fabulous spiritual paradox that when you embrace being your ordinary average self, the joy, peace and love that you've been seeking is already right here, right now. Nothing special. Ordinary average people built the pyramids. Average people rock. Furthermore, incredibly magical things happen in the lives of average people every day.

You don't live the life you deserve. You live the life you *think* you deserve. It's not earned – it's Consciousness.

Prepare <u>yourself</u> and the opportunity will come. Work on your Consciousness and be ready to walk through the open doors when the appear. Sometimes the open door is one that you built yourself, but make sure every door you build is one that you will enjoy walking through and not one that that you think you "should" walk through.

You don't have to passively wait for doors to open. If you see an attractive door, by all means, knock with boldness and courage. Just don't keep smashing your head against the doors that are locked. If they don't want you in there, believe me, that's not a good place for you. What you want is to be surrounded by those who "get you" just the way you are.

A closed mouth never gets fed. Ask directly and specifically for what you want. People are not here to read our minds and everyone is free to say yes or no. ASK. Don't hint or wish or hope - ASK.

Affirm, Believe, Relax, Receive. Strangely, the "relax" part is the hardest for most people. Relaxing is a skill. If you don't have it, study your cat. If you don't know how to play, study your dog.

The better it gets, the better it gets.

My success formula in life is this: Show up, prepared, on time, doing what you said you would do, with a good attitude. Everything else is out of our control.

I don't know much. I only know a few things, but those few things rule the entire Universe. There are no "new" eternal ancient Truths.

DON'T BELIEVE EVERYTHING YOU THINK.

Think about what you are thinking about.

You've so vain, you probably think this talk is about you.

You can make it happen, but you can't make it work.

The #1 rule of dating is this: Don't date people who have contempt for you.

Post a guard at the door of your mind.

There is a common denominator in every tragedy and upset in your life – you were there. This is very good news because if you are the common denominator in the drama, you are the common denominator in every joyous moment, every miracle and every step forward. Focus on that and know that what you focus on increases.

There is SO MUCH good in the world for you! There is so much money, so many eligible people, so many jobs and opportunities, so many homes to live in, so many friendly companions, so much healing and vitality! You must never speak or entertain lack as anything other than a very temporary experience that cannot stay. Our job is to give all the good a place to land by speaking from a place of ever-increasing abundant good. Remember, WE'VE CONSULTED A HIGHER AUTHORITY!

Life is hard for everyone because everyone has a mind that thinks.

The moment you say "never," you've signed up for the event. What you resist, persists. Practice non-resistance as you focus on what you DO want instead of what you don't want.

If you find what you love to do, just stand still and keep doing it anywhere that you can. Eventually you'll rise to the top because most everyone else leaves if they don't get what they want right away. One day you'll look around and notice that you're the only one left. Then, they'll call you a overnight success!

Before you go to war over anything, ask yourself, *"Is that the hill I want to die on?"*

The essence of New Thought is this: the calls are coming from inside the house. No one else is thinking inside our heads.

About once a week it's good to look in the mirror and say, *"I'm onto you. Stop it."*

I call the life of Spirit "Opposite World" because it is the exact opposite of the world of flesh. Everything I ever tried to accomplish turned out the extreme opposite. When I tried to make money, I ended up in debt. When I tried to get love, they ran from me like my hair was on fire. When I tried to promote my work, every room I spoke in was empty. When I tried to be fit and healthy, I was sick and fat all the time. My life didn't start until I completely gave up in failure and financial ruin and surrendered my mess to God. Now, my mess has become my message.

Quantum leaps are a very rough ride and whatever ground is covered is often easily lost. I teach penguin steps because they are more easily achieved, maintained and sustained. Penguins take tiny steps but make it all the way across the Antarctic and back. They don't get impatient and give up the way humans do. Penguin steps are POWERFUL.

Call off the search! Bring in the bloodhounds. Stop the endless auditioning for life. Relax, and let your good find you. If you build it, they will come. If you chase them, they will run.

It's that ONE MIND thing again.

Instead of thinking in violent terms like "breakthrough" and think more in terms of dissolving or neutralizing. Be gentle with yourself.

Learn to be a gracious receiver – and make it EASY for people to contribute to you, instead of making it difficult.

I'm no longer curious about things that will upset me.

When your ego goes into attack mode against them, remember: *"just like me."*

It is not true that *"when you know better you do better."* The vast history of mankind speaks to the contrary of this. Our biggest regrets come when we are able to say, *"I knew I shouldn't have _____"* but we did it anyway. The diet industry makes billions because we do things we know better than to do. It does no good to pretend that knowing leads to doing. What leads to doing is a DECISION based on what we know. Knowledge is not power – it's only *potential* power. And the most helpful doing is when we remove guilt from the equation and simply make choices that will lead us to our goal in ways that are for the highest good of all concerned. And it's very difficult to do this without Divine Aid and Grace. Self-will really only goes so far for most of us and then we rebound back to the sabotaging habits of the ego. It takes more than knowledge and will power. It takes a decision to SURRENDER that knowledge to the Grace of God to help us make better choices.

Constructive criticism is a myth. That's like saying "helpful attack."

Be careful what you activate in others because whatever you activate in them, you will then have to deal with. If you complain about your mate to your friend, you've activated judgment in your friend. Now, when you forgive your mate, your friend may never get back to liking them. What YOU activate, you will have to deal with. Be careful what you activate in others and focus on activating the things that you WANT to deal with.

We're never giving up control. We only give up the illusion of control.

It's so freeing when you notice that people do exactly what they want to do. And people like you or they don't. When we get this, we can just be ourselves and let people come and go as they please – because they will anyhow. It's called, *"releasing the hostages."*

It's surprising how often I find people who want to reap before they will sow. Then, they wonder why they live in such struggle and lack. You cannot eat your pumpkin seeds and still grow pumpkins. But if you sow your one seed, you may grow a vine that produces a dozen pumpkins full of seeds. There is a specific order to the Universe. Sow, THEN reap – not the other way around. This is not "giving to get" – it's sowing and reaping. It's a natural law. We cannot out-give God.

A "get" mentality is not a receptive mentality. If you try to get the best deal out of someone while receiving the most value, that is exactly what will be reflected back to you. The Universe will get the most out of you, while giving you the least. If you do not pay top dollar to people for their goods and services, then you will not receive top dollar for yours. If you steal downloaded music, don't be surprised if people are stealing from you all the time – even if what they are stealing is your time, attention and energy. The Universal accounts always get balanced. It's Universal Law. At restaurants, I always tip based on Who I am, never on the service given – because I understand that everything that I give is sowing a seed to MY own prosperity and thriving. It has nothing to do with the other person. They will reap according to what THEY sow and that is none of my business.

It's just a thought, and a thought can be changed.

Never argue for your limitations. Never argue for the limitations of others.

How great are you willing to LET your life get?

Without a strong no, you've got a weak yes.

Look for the open doors.

Loss happens in life – it happens to all of us. Metaphysics does not prevent loss. Everything here is temporary. But, if you want to have peace, STOP FOCUSING ON WHAT YOU HAD, AND START FOCUSING ON WHAT YOU HAVE.

We can waste a lot of time off on the side of the road trying to figure out why or how we got so lost. Or we can simply reprogram the GPS and get right back on the highlighted route. Assigning blame, guilt or shame just makes for a dour journey.

FAVORITE A COURSE IN MIRACLES QUOTES

I BECAME A STUDENT OF THE COURSE in 1984 through a New Though church that I was attending at the time. I have many favorite quotes but I wanted to include here the ones I have used most in my classes and lectures over the years.

ON FAITH

Why is it strange to you that faith can move mountains? This is indeed a little feat for such a power. – T pg. 451

The children of God are entitled to the perfect comfort that comes from perfect trust. Until they achieve this, they waste themselves and their true creative powers on useless attempts to make themselves more comfortable by inappropriate means. – T pg. 22

This is the time for faith. You let this goal be set for you. That was an act of faith. Do not abandon faith, now that the rewards of faith are being introduced. –T pg. 363

What could you not accept, if you but knew that everything that happens, all events, past, present and to come, are gently planned by One Whose only purpose is your good? – T pg. 255

We will not let the thoughts of the world hold us back. We will not let the beliefs of the world tell us that what God would have us do is impossible. Instead, we will try to recognize that only what God would have us do is possible. We will also try to understand that only what God would have us do is what we want to do. – WB pg. 71

If there are plans to make, you will be told. – T pg. 255

No evidence will convince you of the truth of what you do not want. –T pg. 333

Do you really believe you can plan for your safety and joy better than He can? You need be neither careful nor careless; you need merely cast your cares upon Him because He careth for you. You are His care because He loves you. – T pg. 88-89

Remember that no one is where he is by accident, and chance plays no part in God's plan. –M pg. 26

ON CREATING

You see what you expect, and you expect what you invite. Your perception is the result of your invitation, coming to you as you sent for it. Whose manifestation would you see? Of whose presence would you be convinced? For you will believe in what you manifest, and as you look out so will you see in. Two ways of looking at the world are in your mind, and your perception will reflect the guidance you have chosen. – T pg. 230

Without a clear-cut, positive goal, set at the outset, the situation just seems to happen, and makes no sense until it has already happened. Then you look back at it, and try to piece together what it must have meant. And you will be wrong . . . No goal was set with which to bring the means in line. And now the only judgment left to make is whether or not the ego likes it; is it acceptable, or does it call for vengeance? – T pg. 366

The clarification of the goal belongs at the beginning, for it is this which will determine the outcome . . . the ego does not know what it wants to come of the situation. It is aware of what it does not want, but only that. It has no positive goal at all. – T pg. 366

This is the only thing that you need do for vision,

happiness, release from pain and the complete escape from sin, all to be given you. Say only this, but mean it with no reservations, for here the power of salvation lies: *I **am** responsible for what I see. I choose the feelings I experience, and I decide upon the goal I would achieve. And everything that seems to happen to me I ask for, and receive as I have asked.* –T pg. 448

Now you must learn that only infinite patience produces immediate results. –T pg. 88

It cannot be that it is hard to do the task that Christ appointed you to do, since it is He Who does it. – T pg. 518

When you come to the place where the branch in the road is quite apparent, you cannot go ahead. You must go either one way or the other. For now if you go straight ahead, the way you went before you reached the branch, you will go nowhere. The whole purpose of coming this far was to decide which branch you will take now. The way you came no longer matters. It can no longer serve. No one who reaches this far can make the wrong decision, although he can delay. And there is no part of the journey that seems more hopeless and futile than standing where the road branches, and not deciding on which way to go. – T pg. 477

ON GUILT & JUDGMENT

The Holy Spirit is not delayed in His teaching by your mistakes. He can be held back only by your unwillingness to let them go. – WB pg. 167

The attraction of guilt is found in sin, not error. Sin will be repeated because of the attraction . . . An error, on the other hand, is not attractive. What you see clearly as a mistake you want corrected. – T pg. 404

Guilt is a sure sign that your thinking is unnatural. –T pg. 84

In order to judge anything rightly, one would have to be fully aware of an inconceivably wide range of things; past, present and to come. One would have to recognize in advance all the effects of his judgment on everyone and everything involved in them in any way. And one would have to be certain there is no distortion in his perception, so that his judgment would be wholly fair to everyone on whom it rests now and in the future. Who is in a position to do this? Who except in grandiose fantasies would claim this for himself? –M pg. 27

You are not really capable of being tired, but you are very capable of wearying yourself. The strain of constant judgment is virtually intolerable. It is curious that an ability so debilitating would be so deeply cherished. – T pg. 47

On Giving and Receiving

The cost of giving *is* receiving. – T pg. 275

Who understands what giving means must laugh at the idea of sacrifice. – T pg. 354-355

To spirit getting is meaningless and giving is all. –T pg. 73

If paying is equated with getting, you will set the price low but demand a high return. You will have forgotten, however, that to price is to value, so that your return is in proportion to your judgment of worth. If paying is associated with giving it cannot be perceived as loss, and the reciprocal relationship of giving and receiving will be recognized. The price will then be set high, because of the value of the return. The price for getting is to lose sight of value, making it inevitable that you will not value what you receive. Valuing it little, you will not appreciate it and you will not want it. – T pg. 165

ON THE MIND

Decisions are continuous. You do not always know when you are making them. But with a little practice with the ones you recognize, a set begins to form which will see you through the rest. – T pg. 625

It is much more helpful to remind you that you do not guard your thoughts carefully enough . . . I cannot let you leave your mind unguarded, or you will not be able to help me. –T pg. 31

Simplicity is very difficult for twisted minds. –T pg. 272

You would not excuse insane behavior on your part by saying you could not help it. Why should you condone insane thinking? – T pg. 29

You may still complain about fear, but you nevertheless persist in making yourself fearful. I have already indicated that you cannot ask me to release you from fear. I know it does not exist, but you do not. If I intervened between your thoughts and their results, I would be tampering with a basic law of cause and effect; the most fundamental law there is. I would hardly help you if I depreciated the power of your own thinking . . . It is much more helpful to remind you that you do not guard your thoughts carefully enough. –T pg. 31

The correction of fear is your responsibility . . . you are much too tolerant of mind wandering, and are passively condoning your mind's miscreations. – T pg. 29

This is a course in mind training. All learning involves attention and study at some level. Some of the later parts of the course rest too heavily on these earlier sections not to require their careful study. – T pg. 16

To learn this course requires willingness to question every

value that you hold. Not one can be kept hidden and obscure but will jeopardize your learning. No belief is neutral. – T pg. 499

Undermining the ego's thought system must be perceived as painful, even though this is anything but true. Babies scream in rage if you take away a knife or scissors, although they may well harm themselves if you do not. In this sense you are still a baby. You have no sense of real self-preservation, and are likely to decide that you need precisely what would hurt you most. – T pg. 57

ON DEALING WITH PROBLEMS

I do not know what anything, including this, means. And so I do not know how to respond to it. And I will not use my own past learning as the light to guide me now. – T pg. 298

Trials are but lessons that you failed to learn presented once again, so where you made a faulty choice before you now can make a better one, and thus escape all pain that what you chose before has brought you. –T pg. 666

Be certain that any answer to a problem the Holy Spirit solves will always be one in which no one loses. – T pg. 539

I must have decided wrongly, because I am not at peace. I made the decision myself, but I can decide otherwise. I want to decide otherwise, because I want to be at peace. I do not feel guilty, because the Holy Spirit will undo all the consequences of my wrong decision if I will let Him. I choose to let Him, by allowing Him to decide for God for me. – T pg. 90

It is essential to realize that all defenses _do_ what they would defend. T pg. 359

When anything seems to you to be a source of fear, when any situation strikes you with terror and makes your body tremble and the cold sweat of fear comes over it, remember it is always for one reason; the ego has perceived it as a symbol of fear, a sign of sin and death . . . Give it to Him to judge for you, and say: *Take this from me and look upon it, judging it for me. Let me not see it as a sign of sin and death, nor use it for destruction. Teach me how* **not** *to make of it an obstacle to peace, but let You use it for me, to facilitate its coming.* –T pg. 419

ON OUR FUNCTION AND BEING HELPFUL

I am here only to be truly helpful. I am here to represent Him Who sent me. I do not have to worry about what to say or what to do, because He Who sent me will direct me. I am content to be wherever He wishes, knowing He goes there with me. I will be healed as I let Him teach me to heal. – T. pg 28

To empathize does not mean to join in suffering. – T pg. 330

You are altogether irreplaceable in the Mind of God. No one else can fill your part of it, and while you leave your part of it empty your eternal place merely waits for your return. –T pg. 179

The truth about you is so lofty that nothing unworthy of God is worthy of you. – T pg. 177

ON JOY AND HAPPINESS

To heal is to make happy. I have told you think how many opportunities you have had to gladden yourself, and how many you have refused. This is the same as telling you that you have refused to heal yourself. – T pg. 72

There is a way of living in the world that is not here, although it seems to be. You do not change appearance, though you smile more frequently. – WB pg. 291

There is no difference between love and joy. – T pg. 72

The Holy Spirit needs a happy learner, in whom His mission can be happily accomplished. You who are steadfastly devoted to misery must first recognize that you are miserable and not happy. The Holy Spirit cannot teach without this contrast, for you believe that misery *is* happiness. – T pg 272

The opposite of joy is depression. When your learning promotes depression instead of joy, you cannot be listening to God's joyous Teacher and learning His lessons. – T pg. 154

If you inspire joy and others react to you with joy, even though you are not experiencing joy yourself there must be something in you that is capable of producing it. If it is in you and can produce joy, and if you see that it does produce joy in others, you must be dissociating it in yourself. – T pg. 173

Everyone teaches, and teaches all the time . . . Once you have developed a thought system of any kind, you live by it and teach it. – T pg. 91

He speaks for the Kingdom of God, which *is* joy. Following Him is therefore the easiest thing in the world, and the only thing that is easy, because it is not of this world. It is therefore natural. – T pg. 136

ON GOD, JESUS, YOU & THE HOLY SPIRIT

Fear of the Will of God is one of the strangest beliefs the human mind has ever made. –T pg. 160

A sense of separation from God is the only lack you really need correct. –T pg. 14

You are the work of God, and His work is wholly lovable

and wholly loving. This is how one should think of herself in her heart because this is what she is. – T pg. 9

You can wait, delay, paralyze yourself, or reduce your creativity almost to nothing. But you cannot abolish it. You can destroy your medium of communication, but not your potential. You did not create yourself. –T pg. 12

There is no emptiness in you. Because of your likeness to your Creator you are creative. No child of God can lose this ability . . . –T pg. 17

Simply do this: Be still, and lay aside all thoughts of what you are and what God is; all concepts you have learned about the world; all images you hold about yourself. Empty your mind of everything it thinks is either true or false, or good or bad, of every thought it judges worthy, and all the ideas of which it is ashamed. Hold onto nothing. Do not bring with you one thought the past has taught, nor one belief you ever learned before from anything. Forget this world, forget this course, and come with wholly empty hands unto your God. –T pg. 360

There is nothing about me that you cannot attain. I have nothing that does not come from God. The difference between us now is that I have nothing else. This leaves me in a state which is only potential in you. – T pg. 7

Some bitter idols have been made of him who would be only brother to the world. Forgive him your illusions. – M pg. 88

Is he God's only Helper? No, indeed. For Christ takes many forms with different names until their oneness can be recognized. – M pg. 88

I can be entrusted with your body and your ego only because this enables you not to be concerned with them, and lets me teach you their unimportance. I could not understand their importance to you if I had not once been tempted to believe in them myself. – T pg. 56

We are trying today to undo your definition of God and replace it with His Own. – WB pg. 113

ON GUIDANCE

Say to the Holy Spirit only, *"Decide for me,"* and it is done. – T pg. 278

It will never happen that you must make decisions for yourself. You are not bereft of help, and Help that knows the answer. – T pg. 276

If you are trusting in your own strength, you have every reason to be apprehensive, anxious and fearful. –WB pg. 75

Ask Him very specifically: *What would you have me do? Where would you have me go? What would you have me say, and to whom?*

It is only because you think that you can run some little part, or deal with certain aspects of your life alone, that the guidance of the Holy Spirit is limited. – T pg. 298

The habit of engaging with God and His creations is easily made if you actively refuse to let your mind slip away. The problem is not one of concentration; it is the belief that no one, including yourself is worth consistent effort. –T pg. 64

It is, perhaps, not easy to perceive that self-initiated plans are but defenses . . . – T pg. 254

The mind engaged in planning for itself is occupied in setting up control of future happenings. It does not think it will be provided for, unless it makes its own provisions . . . the mind that plans is thus refusing to allow for change. – T pg. 254

You who cannot even control yourself should hardly aspire to control the universe. – T pg. 234

This is your major problem now. You still make up your mind, and *then* decide to ask what you should do. – T pg. 626

ON GRACE

Grace is the natural state of every child of God When he is not in a state of grace, he is out of his natural environment and does not function well. – T pg. 136

ON RELATIONSHIPS

When you love someone you have perceived him as he is, and this makes it possible for you to know him. Until you first perceive him as he is you cannot know him. – T pg. 41

Whenever you meet anyone, remember it is a holy encounter. As you see him you will see yourself. As you treat him you will treat yourself. As you think of him you will think of yourself. Never forget this, for in him you will find yourself or lose yourself. Whenever two Sons of God meet, they are given another chance at salvation. –T pg. 142

What you perceive in others you are strengthening in yourself. – T pg. 80

You can place any relationship under His care and be sure that it will not result in pain, if you offer Him your willingness to have it serve no need but His. All the guilt in it arise from your use of it. All the love from His. Do not, then, be afraid to let go your imagined needs, which would destroy the relationship. Your only need is His. Any relationship you would substitute for another has not been offered to the Holy Spirit for His use. – T pg. 313

Whoever is saner at the time the threat is perceived

should remember . . . and say: I desire this holy instant for myself, that I may share it with my brother, whom I love. It is not possible that I can have it without him, or he without me. Yet it is wholly possible for us to share it now. And so I choose this instant as the one to offer to the Holy Spirit, that His blessing may descend on us, and keep us both in peace. –T pg. 384

The ego establishes relationships only to get something. – T pg. 317

This is why you see in both what is not there, and make of both the slaves of vengeance. And why whatever reminds you of your past grievances attracts you, and seems to go by the name of love, not matter how distorted the associations by which you arrive at the connection may be. – T pg. 355

In the unholy relationship, it is not the body of the other with which union is attempted, but the bodies of those who are not there. – T pg. 355

Say, then, to your brother: *I give you to the Holy Spirit as part of myself. I know that you will be released, unless I want to use you to imprison myself. In the name of my freedom I choose your release, because I recognize that we will be released together.* – T pg. 329

The alertness of the ego to the errors of other egos is not the kind of vigilance the Holy Spirit would have you maintain . . . to the ego it is kind and right and good to point out errors and "correct" them. This makes perfect sense to the ego, which is unaware of what errors are and what correction is . . . if you point out the errors of your brother's ego you must be seeing through yours, because the Holy Spirit does not perceive his errors. – T pgs. 166-167

Dream of your brother's kindnesses instead of dwelling in your dreams on his mistakes. Select his thoughtfulness to dream about instead of counting up the hurts he gave. Forgive him his illusions, and give thanks to him for all the helpfulness he gave. And do not brush aside his many gifts because he is not perfect in your dreams. –T pg. 585

When a brother behaves insanely, you can heal him only by perceiving the sanity in him. – T 167

It is not up to you to change your brother, but merely to accept him as he is. – T pg. 167

Any attempt you make to correct a brother means that you believe correction by you is possible, and this can only be the arrogance of the ego. Correction is of God, Who does not know of arrogance. – T pg. 168

For an unholy relationship is based on differences, where each one thinks the other has what he has not. They come together, each to complete himself and rob the other. They stay until there is nothing left to steal, and then move on. And so they wander through a world of strangers, unlike themselves, living with their bodies perhaps under a common roof that shelters neither; in the same room and yet a world apart. A holy relationship starts from a different premise. Each one has looked within and seen no lack. Accepting his completion, he would extend it by joining with another, whole as himself. – T pg. 467

The ego's plan for salvation centers around holding grievances. It maintains that, if someone else spoke or acted differently, if some external circumstance or event were changed, you would be saved. Thus, the source of salvation is constantly perceived as outside yourself. Each grievance you hold is a declaration, and an assertion in which you believe, that says, *"If this were different, I would be saved."* The change of mind necessary for salvation is thus demanded of everyone and everything except yourself. – WB pg. 121

Your patience with your brother is your patience with

yourself. Is not a child of God worth patience? I have shown you infinite patience. – T pg. 88

ON HEALING

The healer who relies on his own readiness is endangering his understanding. You are perfectly safe as long as you are completely unconcerned about your readiness, but maintain a consistent trust in mine. – T pg. 25

The sole responsibility of the miracle worker is to accept the Atonement for himself. – T pg. 25-26

Pride will not produce miracles. – T pg 179

There is an advantage to bringing nightmares into awareness, but only to teach that they are not real, and that anything they contain is meaningless. – T pg. 171

Healing is not a miracle . . . All healing is essentially the release from fear. –T pg. 23

True denial is a powerful protective device. You can and should deny any belief that error can hurt you. This kind of denial is not a concealment but a correction. – T pg. 19

Tolerance for pain may be high, but it is not without limit. Eventually everyone begins to recognize, however dimly, that there *must* be a better way. – T pg. 22

ON THE BODY AND HEALTH

You still have too much faith in the body as a source of strength . . . there is one thing you have never done; you have not utterly forgotten the body . . . you are not asked to let this happen for more than an instant, yet it is in this instant that the miracle of Atonement happens. Afterwards you will see the body again, but never quite the same. And every instant that you spend without awareness of it gives you a different view of it when you return. – T pg. 388

The body's serial adventures, from the time of birth to dying are the theme of every dream the world has ever had. – T pg. 585

Remember that the Holy Spirit interprets the body only as a means of communication. – T pg. 151

The body is in need of no defense. This cannot be too often emphasized. It will be strong and healthy if the mind does not abuse it by assigning it to roles it cannot fill, to purposes beyond its scope, and to exalted aims which it cannot accomplish. – T pg. 253

ON MIRACLES

There is no order of difficulty in miracles. – T pg. 3

Each day should be devoted to miracles. – T pg. 4

The miracle does nothing. All it does is to undo. –T pg. 589

Miracles are expressions of love, but they may not always have observable effects. – T pg. 5

A miracle is never lost. It may touch many people you have not even met, and produce undreamed of changes in situations of which you are not even aware. T pg. 6

Miracles, however, are genuinely interpersonal, and result in true closeness to others. Revelation unites you directly with God. Miracles unite you directly with your brother . . . The miracle is therefore a sign of love among equals. T pg. 7

As you share my unwillingness to accept error in yourself and others, you must join the great crusade to correct it; listen to my voice, learn to undo error and act to correct it. The power to work miracles belongs to you. I will provide the opportunities to do them, but you must be ready and willing. Doing them will bring conviction in the ability, because conviction comes through accomplishment. –T pg. 9

ON CRUCIFIXION AND VICTIM THINKING

The only message of the crucifixion is that you can overcome the cross. Until then you are free to crucify yourself as often as you choose. –T pg. 52

This aspect can grow angry, for the world is wicked and unable to provide the love and shelter innocence deserves. And so this face is often wet with tears at the injustices the world accords to those who would be generous and good. This aspect never makes the first attack. But every day a hundred little things make small assaults upon its innocence, provoking it to irritation, and at last to open insult and abuse . . . Beneath the face of innocence there is a lesson that the concept of the self was made to teach. It is a lesson in a terrible displacement, and a fear so devastating that the face that smiles above it must forever look away, lest it perceive the treachery it hides. The lesson teaches this: *"I am the thing you made of me, and as you look on me, you stand condemned because of what I am."* – T pg.. 656

Many stand guard over their ideas because they want to protect their thought systems as they are, and learning means change. Change is always fearful to the separated, because they cannot conceive of it as a move towards healing the separation. –T pg. 53

Beware of the temptation to perceive yourself unfairly treated. – T pg. 563

You have probably reacted for years as if you were being crucified. This is a marked tendency of the separated, who always refuse to consider what they have done to themselves. –

T. pg 92

As you read the teachings of the Apostles, remember that I told them myself that there was much they would understand later, because they were not wholly ready to follow me at the time. –T pg. 95

I do not call for martyrs but for teachers. –T pg. 95

You who are sometimes sad and sometimes angry; who sometimes feel your just due is not given you, and your best efforts meet with lack of appreciation and even contempt; give up these foolish thoughts! They are too small and meaningless to occupy your holy mind an instant longer. – M pg. 38

ON GRATITUDE AND APPRECIATION

I do not need gratitude, but you need to develop your weakened ability to be grateful, or you cannot appreciate God. –T pg. 95

Gratitude to God becomes the way in which He is remembered, for love cannot be far behind a grateful heart and thankful mind. – T pg. 58

ON THE WORLD

This is an insane world, and do not underestimate the extent of its insanity. There is no area of your perception that it has not touched, and your dream is sacred to you. That is why God placed the Holy Spirit in you, where you placed the dream. – T pg. 271

Beyond this world there is a world I want . . . Our emphasis is not on giving up the world, but on exchanging it for what is far more satisfying, filled with joy, and capable of offering you peace. –WB pg. 235

As a man thinketh, so does he perceive. Therefore, seek not to change the world, but choose to change your mind about the world. Perception is a result and not a cause. And that is why order of difficulty in miracles is meaningless. Everything looked upon with vision is healed and holy. Nothing perceived without it means anything. And where there is no meaning, there is chaos. –T pg. 445

On Peace

I want the peace of God. To say these words is nothing. But to mean these words is everything . . . No one can mean these words and not be healed. –T pg. 348

In reality you are perfectly unaffected by all expressions of lack of love. These can be from yourself and others, from yourself to others, or from others to you. Peace is an attribute in you. You cannot find it outside. – T pg. 18

To be in the Kingdom is merely to focus your full attention on it. – T pg. 117

On Love

You who want peace can find it only by complete forgiveness. – T pg. 13

Love does not conquer all things, but it does set all things right. –T pg. 69

When you want only love you will see nothing else. T pg. 231

On Forgiveness

You who want peace can find it only by complete forgiveness. – T pg. 13

. . . you accept God's forgiveness by extending it to others. –T pg. 4

To forgive is merely to remember only the loving thoughts you gave in the past, and those that were given you. All the rest must be forgotten. Forgiveness is a selective remembering, based not on your selection. –T pg. 354

OTHER COURSE QUOTES

You must have noticed an outstanding characteristic of every end that the ego has accepted as its own. When you have achieved it, *it has not satisfied you*. This is why the ego is forced to shift ceaselessly from one goal to another, so that you will continue to hope it can yet offer you something. – T pg. 155

The one wholly true thought one can hold about the past is that it is not here. –WB pg. 13

"Except ye become as little children" means that unless you fully recognize your complete dependence on God, you cannot know the real power of the Son in his true relationship with the Father. – T pg. 12

Jacob Glass

<u>FAVORITE BIBLE QUOTES</u>

FOR ME, THE BIBLE IS NOT A HISTORY BOOK nor are the stories in it meant to be taken literally. Yet, there is great wisdom and comfort to be found there if that is what you are looking for and want to find. Here are some of the ones that have helped me on my journey through this life.

And he said to me, *My grace is sufficient for thee: for my strength is made perfect in weakness.* Most gladly therefore will I rather glory in my infirmities, that the power of Christ may rest upon me. – 2 Corinthians 11:24

Trust in the Lord with all thine heart; and lean not unto thine own understanding. In all thy ways acknowledge him, and he shall direct by paths. – Proverbs 3: 5-6

Finally brethren, whatsoever things are true, whatsoever things are just, whatsoever things are pure, whatsoever things are lovely, whatsoever things are of good report; if there be any virtue, and if there be any praise, think on these things. – Philippians 4:8

He healeth the broken in heart, and bindeth up their wounds. – Psalm 147:3

Now that I speak in respect of want: for I have learned, in whatsoever state I am, therewith to be content. I know both how to be abased, and I know how to abound: everywhere and in all things I am instructed both to be full and to be hungry, both to abound and to suffer need. I can do all things through Christ which strengtheneth me. – Phillipians 4:11-13

Come unto me all ye that labor and are heavy laden, and I will give you rest. – Matthew 11:28

And Jabez called on the God of Israel, saying, "Oh that

thou wouldst bless me indeed, and enlarge my coast, and that thine hand might be with me, and that thou wouldst keep me from evil, that it may not grieve me!" And God granted him that which he requested. – 1 Chronicles 4:10

Bring ye all the tithes into the storehouse, that there may be meat in mine house, and prove me now herewith, saith the Lord of hosts, if I will not open you the windows of heaven, and pour you out a blessing, that there shall not be room to receive it. – Malachi 3:10

I have been young, and now am old; yet have I not seen the righteous forsaken, nor his seed begging bread.

And his disciples asked him, saying, Master, who did sin, this man, or his parents, that he was born blind? Jesus answered, Neither hath this man sinned, nor his parents: but that the works of God should be made manifest in him. – John 9:2-3

Therefore doth my Father love me, because I lay down my life, that I might take it up again. No man taketh it from me, but I lay it down of myself. I have power to lay it down, and I have power to take it again. This commandment have I received of my Father. – John 10:17-18

The thief cometh not, but for to steal, and to kill, and to destroy: I am come that they might have life, and that they might have it more abundantly. – John 9:10

He giveth power to the faint; and to them that have no might he increaseth strength. Even the youths shall faint and be weary, and the young men shall utterly fall: But they that wait upon the Lord shall renew their strength; they shall mount up with wings as eagles; they shall run, and not be weary; and they shall walk, and not faint. – Isaiah 40:29-31

And Jesus said unto him, No man, having put his hand to the plow, and looking back, is fit for the kingdom of God. –

Luke 9:62

And he said unto them, Where is your faith? – Luke 8:25

And he said to the woman, Thy faith has saved thee; go in peace. – Luke 7:50

Therefore I say unto you, Take no thought for your life, what ye shall eat; neither for the body, what ye shall put on. The life is more than meat, and the body is more than raiment. Consider the ravens: for they neither sow nor reap; which neither have storehouse nor barn; and God feedeth them: how much more are ye better than the fowls? And which of you with taking thought can add to his stature one cubit? – Luke 12:22-25

Consider the lilies how they grow: they toil not, they spin not; and yet I say unto you, that Solomon in all his glory was not arrayed like one of these. If then God so clothe the grass which is today in the field, and tomorrow is cast in the oven; how much more will he clothe you, O ye of little faith? – Luke 12:27-28

. . . and your Father knoweth that ye have need of these things. But rather seek ye the kingdom of God; and all these things shall be added unto you. Fear not, little flock; for it is your Father's good pleasure to give you the kingdom. – Luke 12:30-32

And when he was demanded of the Pharisees, when the kingdom of God should come, he answered them and said, The kingdom of God cometh not with observation: Neither shall they say, Lo here! Or, lo there! for, behold, the kingdom of God is within you. – Luke 17:20-21

A new commandment I give unto you, That ye love one another; as I have loved you, that ye also love one another. By this shall all men know that ye are my disciples, if ye have love one to another. – John 13:34-35

Ask, and it shall be given you; seek, and ye shall find; knock, and it shall be opened unto you: For every one that asketh receiveth; and he that seeketh findeth; and to him that knocketh it shall be opened. – Matthew 7:7-8

With men this is impossible; but with God all things are possible. – Matthew 19:26

Did ye never read in the Scriptures, The stone which the builders rejected, the same is become the head of the corner: this is the Lord's doing, and it is marvelous in our eyes? – Matthew 21:42

Verily I say unto you, If ye have faith, and doubt not, ye shall not only do this which is done to the fig tree, but also if ye shall say unto this mountain, Be thou removed, and be thou cast into the sea; it shall be done. And all things, whatsoever ye shall ask in prayer, believing, ye shall receive. – Matthew 21:21-22

For John came neither eating and drinking, and they say, He hath a devil. The Son of man came eating and drinking, and they say, Behold a man gluttonous, and a winebibber, a friend of publicans and sinners. But wisdom is justified of her children . . . I thank thee, O Father, Lord of heaven and earth, because thou hast hidden these things from the wise and prudent, and hast revealed them unto babes. – Matthew 11:18-25

Not that which goeth into the mouth defileth a man; but that which cometh out of the mouth, this defileth a man. – Matthew 15:11

Woe unto you, scribes and Pharisees, hypocrites! For ye make clean the outside of the cup and of the platter, but within they are full of extortion and excess Thou blind Pharisee, cleanse first that which is within the cup and platter, that the outside of them may be clean also. Woe unto you, scribes and

Pharisees, hypocrites! For ye are like unto whited sepulchers, which indeed appear beautiful outward, but are within full of dead men's bones, and of all uncleanness. – Matthew 23:25-27

Whence hath this man this wisdom, and these mighty works? Is not this the carpenter's son? Is not his mother called Mary? And his brethren, James, and Joses, and Simon, and Judas? And his sisters, are they not all with us? Whence then hath this man all these things? And they were offended in him. But Jesus said unto them, A prophet is not without honor, save in his own country, and in his own house. – Matthew 13:54-57

For I am persuaded, that neither death, nor life, nor angels, nor principalities, nor powers, nor things present, nor things to come, nor height, nor depth, nor any other creature, shall be able to separate us from the love of God. – Romans 8:38-39

Ye are the light of the world. A city that is set on a hill cannot be hid. Neither do men light a candle and put it under a bushel, but on a candlestick; and it giveth light unto all that are in the house. Let your light so shine before men, that they may see your good works, and glorify your Father which is in heaven. – Matthew 5:14-16

Neither do men put new wine into old bottles: else the bottles break, and the wine runneth out, and the bottles perish: but they put new wine into new bottles and both are preserved. –Matthew 9:17

But I say unto you, Love your enemies, bless them that curse you, do good to them that hate you, and pray for them which despitefully use you, and persecute you: that ye may be the children of your Father which is in heaven: for he maketh his sun to rise on the evil and on the good, and sendeth rain on the just and the unjust. For if ye love them which love you, what reward have ye? Do not even the publicans the same? And if ye salute your brethren only, what do ye more than others? Do not even the publicans so? Be ye therefore perfect, even as your Father which is in heaven is perfect. – Matthew 5:44-48

Make a joyful noise unto God, all ye lands. – Psalm 66:1

If any of you lack wisdom, let him ask of God, that giveth to all men liberally, and upbraideth not; and it shall be given him. But let him ask in faith, nothing wavering. For he that wavereth is like a wave of the sea driven with the wind and tossed. – James 1:5-6

But be ye doers of the word, and not hearers only, deceiving your own selves. – James 1:22

But if ye are led of the Spirit, ye are not under the law. – Galatians 5:18

And let us not be weary in well-doing: for in due season we shall reap, if we faint not. – Galatians 6:9

But when thou doest alms, let not thy left hand know what thy right hand doeth: that thine alms may be in secret: and thy Father which seeth in secret himself shall reward thee openly. – Matthew 6:3-4

The Lord is my light and my salvation; whom shall I fear? The Lord is the strength of my life; of whom shall I be afraid? – Psalm 27:1

When thou sadist, Seek ye my face; my heart said unto thee, Thy face, Lord, will I seek. – Psalm 27:8

Wait on the Lord: be of good courage, and he shall strengthen thine heart: wait, I say, on the Lord. – Psalm 27:14

Father, I thank thee that thou hast heard me. And I knew that thou hearest me always: but because of the people which stand by I said it, that they may believe that thou hast sent me.

– John 11:41-42

For they loved the praise of men more than the praise of God. – John 12:43

My son, despise not the chastening of the Lord; neither be weary of his correction: for whom the Lord loveth he correcteth; even as a father the son in whom he delighteth. – Proverbs 3:11-12

I will pour my spirit unto you, I will make known my words unto you. – Proverbs 1:23

For my thoughts are not your thoughts, neither are your ways my ways, saith the Lord. For as the heavens are higher than the earth, so are my ways higher than your ways, and my thoughts than your thoughts. – Isaiah 55:8-9

So shall my word be that goeth forth out of my mouth: it shall not return unto me void, but it shall accomplish that which I please, and it shall prosper in the thing whereto I sent it. – Isaiah 55:11

FAVORITE NEVILLE GODDARD QUOTES

NEVILLE GODDARD IS ONE OF MY FAVORITE TEACHERS and I didn't want to miss the opportunity to share some of his wisdom with you.

The seemingly harmless habit of "talking to yourself" is the most fruitful form of prayer. A mental argument with the subjective image of another is the surest way to pray for an argument.

Imagination is the beginning of creation. You imagine what you desire, and then you believe it to be true.

Imagining novel solutions to ever more complex problems is far more noble than to run from problems.

When man solves the mystery of imagining, he will have discovered the secret of causation, and that is: Imagining creates reality. Therefore, the man who is aware of what he is imagining knows what he is creating; realizes more and more that the drama of life is imaginal not physical.

Prayer is the art of assuming the feeling of being and having that which you want.

Whatever you suggest with confidence is law to the subjective mind; it is under obligation to objectify that which you mentally affirm.

Therefore, if you dwell on difficulties, barriers or delay, the subconscious, by its very non-selective nature, accepts the feeling of difficulties and obstacles as your request and proceeds to produce them in your outer world.

ABOUT THE AUTHOR

Jacob Glass is a spiritual teacher, author, and non-denominational minister. He has been teaching and writing full-time since 1990 throughout Southern California where he resides.

For dates and locations of classes and lectures, resources, inspirational quotes, blogs and information on his CD's and mp3 recordings, please see his website: www.jacobglass.com

CPSIA information can be obtained at www.ICGtesting.com
Printed in the USA
LVOW04s1040161214

419023LV00022B/465/P